*Literature
and Materials
for Sightsinging*

Holt, Rinehart and Winston Consulting Editor in Music:
Allan W. Schindler,
Eastman School of Music

Senior Project Editor	Lester A. Sheinis
Copy Editor	Virginia Newes
Production Manager	Nancy Myers
Art Director	Louis Scardino
Text Design	Arthur Ritter
Page Makeup	Marion Feigl
Typography	Maryland Linotype Composition
Music Engraving	MusiGraph

Literature and Materials for Sightsinging

Richard P. DeLone
Indiana University

Holt, Rinehart and Winston

New York   Chicago   San Francisco   Dallas   Montreal   Toronto   London   Sydney

To Sarah

Library of Congress Cataloging in Publication Data

DeLone, Richard Peter.
  Literature and materials for sightsinging.

  1. Sightsinging. I. Title.
MT870.D374   784.9′4   79–27606
ISBN 0–03–044626–0

Acknowledgments

For the use of copyrighted materials, the author of this book wishes to acknowledge the following:

1. Dominick Argento. *Letters from Composers* (Franz Schubert, *To a Friend*). Copyright © 1971 by Boosey & Hawkes, Inc. Reprinted by permission.
2. Béla Bartók. *Mikrokosmos.* Copyright 1940 by Hawkes & Son (London) Ltd. Copyright © renewed 1967. Reprinted by permission of Boosey & Hawkes, Inc.
3. Béla Bartók. *Concerto for Orchestra.* Copyright 1946 by Hawkes & Son (London) Ltd. Copyright © renewed 1973. Reprinted by permission of Boosey & Hawkes, Inc.

4. Luigi Dallapiccola. *Cinque Frammenti di Saffo.* By permission of the Edizioni Suvini Zerboni, Milano. Reprinted by permission of Boosey & Hawkes, Inc., Sole Agents.
5. Lukas Foss. From "Sechzehnter Januar" from *Time Cycle* by Lukas Foss. Copyright © 1960, 1962 by Carl Fischer, Inc. International copyright secured. All rights reserved. Reproduced by permission of the publisher.

(Acknowledgments are continued on page 414.)

Preface

Like many sightsinging instructors, I have rarely been able to find enough variety of approach or sufficient materials in any single source. As a result, a great deal of time in preparation has been spent gathering material and making it available for students. This text provides materials for sightsinging that reflect the gamut of music literature from plainchant to the twentieth century, and include solo and ensemble, accompanied and unaccompanied selections. Such an approach is consistent with many current undergraduate programs that involve the coordinated study of theory and music literature–history. This text, while *not* a system in itself, introduces several practice analytic procedures that reflect existing pedagogical approaches.* The extent to which these are made a basis for continued practice, however, is left to the discretion of the individual instructor, and only sufficient illustration to present and reinforce such procedures occurs here.

The appended exercises are included by way of practice for the examples found in the historical-stylistic units. In general, the exercises are short. It has been my observation that most students are far more engaged by real music than by made-up materials.

I wish to thank the following reviewers: Bruno Amato, California State University at Fullerton; Shirley Ann Bean, University of Missouri at Kansas City; Emily Brink, University of Illinois; Thomas Brosh, University of North Carolina; David Childs, Wichita State University; Gene J. Cho, North Texas State University; Burt L. Fenner, Pennsylvania State University; Graham H. Phipps, Colorado State University; Kenneth R. Rumery, Northern Arizona University; Julia Shnebly-Black, Georgia State University, Charles E. Stevens, East Carolina University; James Stewart, Ohio University; Allen Winold, Indiana University; Asher G. Zlotnik.

R.P.DeL.

---

* See the Appendix of Supplementary Exercises, page 389.

CONTENTS

Introduction

Many students, indeed many instructors of sightsinging, are unclear about both the need for and the goals of sightsinging courses. Instead of representing a vital concomitant of musicianship, sightsinging often stands for a dull or meaningless course or sequence of courses fulfilling degree requirements—courses to be put up with instead of participated in and profited from. As a result of such misunderstanding by students (and instructors), a valuable tool for developing aural acuity is often misused or overlooked entirely.

The goals of systematic, practiced study of sightsinging are (1) to develop the ability to scan a line or score and hear it with the mind's ear *without* actually sounding the music, and (2) to develop the ability to render vocally at sight music of a wide variety of styles, genres, and levels of difficulty, producing a good approximation of the pace, rhythm, melody, structure, and style of a given passage.

Although ear training and sightsinging are generally treated as separate activities, most instructors agree that the two skills are highly interdependent, ability in one usually indicating ability in the other. For that reason it is important for students to be aware of the relation of sightsinging skill to the ability to use the most precious instrument of all musicians, the ear. Mastery of sightsinging has probably occurred when one has learned "to sing with the ear and hear with the voice." It is to such a goal that these materials are geared.

Singing

Fortunately God did not intend all of us to be singers. In disclaiming any vocal aptitude or inclination many of us ignore one of the most natural resources that we have, namely, a voice, and in most cases the ability, assuming a modest effort, to produce an acceptable vocal sound. Musicians communicate musical ideas through singing, almost as nonmusicians communicate by talking. Our voices are built-in tools for sharing and exchanging ideas about such essential business as phrasing and articulation, recalling figures, themes and motives, intoning rhythms, and for a variety of musical activities that are often more easily and practically undertaken without the use of an instrument. Sightsinging helps beginning musicians to be at ease with the voice as a tool; such natural and spontaneous singing has little relation to the kind of highly developed vocal production demanded of vocal specialists. Related to the use of the voice intended here is the kind of inner singing, often completely silent, that is so important to composers and conductors, for whom the capacity to hear with the mind is essential.

Mode of Vocalization

While this text proposes several kinds of vocalization in the course of its four units, no single system such as the fixed or moveable *do* is advocated throughout, and the decision regarding mode of performance is left to the instructor and the student. However, it is important for musicians to be familiar with the kinds of vocalization that have become more or less standard. With that in mind, suggestions for vocalization are made at various points. For example, Unit Two, which deals with passages from plainchant through Monteverdi, seems expressly appropriate for singing with fixed *do*. Instructors and students who have a strong commitment to one or the other type of performance should use it as long as doing so provides a natural, unforced way of intoning. Singing diatonic music using solfège is an example of a natural and musical way of vocalizing; rendering a highly modulatory Wagnerian melody in scale degree numbers is not.

Uses of This Book

This book is designed for use over a two-year span. Unit One begins with 80 simple, folk-oriented melodies and duos that serve as warm-up materials and present, in the main, minimal problems for nonsingers and students who have done little singing at sight.

Units One and Two form the core of the book and are well suited to programs involving the coordinated study of music literature-history and theory. Units One and Two are intended primarily for the first year, while Units Three and Four should be used as the basis for the second year. However, some teachers and students will undoubtedly want to sample Units Three and Four during the first year, especially the twentieth-century and jazz materials. The solo examples should be used concurrently with the duo or ensemble materials: it is not intended that all of the solo materials be completed before the ensemble examples at the close of each part are undertaken.

The units form a progression from simple to difficult that is consistent with stylistic evolution in music history. The examples within each stylistic unit are arranged in historical order and grouped by composer. Treble, bass, and alto clefs are used in Unit One. The tenor clef is introduced in Unit Two.

Simple meter only is used in Unit One, compound meter is introduced in Unit Two, and mixed meters are found with increasing frequency during the remainder of the text. Ameter occurs in the final unit. Care has been taken to introduce gradually both the visual complexities of rhythmic notation and the various levels of syncopation. Unit One involves little syncopation; in Unit Two syncopation appears in increasing difficulty. Rhythm in general constitutes the most challenging parameter of Unit One, since most students have had little experience performing some of the patterns, such as, hemiola, that are common in early music. The preparatory rhythmic drill in Unit One is therefore of particular importance.

The preparatory rhythmic exercises related to each section appear in a group at the beginning of each part. It is not necessary to complete all the exercises before the musical examples are attempted. To facilitate the reinforcement of exercises with examples from music literature, examples particularly suited to the application of particular problems are given following each exercise. Instructors and students are encouraged to invent similar exercises of their own to supplement the ones in the book. Exercises designed to be helpful in approaching various reading problems—some concentrated on a single aspect of reading, others of more general application—are provided in the Appendix. Relevant exercises are also cited at the beginning of each unit. A number of exercises are cited several times and should be used for concentrated practice of special problems as they occur in the literature.

Suggestions for Practice

Like any musical skill, sightsinging demands continuing, rigorous practice. Most students will find it necessary to plan at least 30 minutes practice time for sightsinging several times each week.

The productiveness of practice or class reading sessions can be enhanced by the development of good reading habits and a simple routine for preparing to read an example. When you read, be sure that the music is sufficiently aligned with eye level so that you do not have to bend or slouch to maintain eye contact with it. Try to keep your eyes moving ahead of the notes being performed. There is no gain in continuing to focus on a note already being sung. In other words, *read ahead.* A good way to insure doing this is to cover the measure being performed with a card or with your hand. This forces you to look ahead, and reading ahead is essential to competent sightsinging.

Keep moving. We all make mistakes when we sight-read. Remember, as a rule, sight-reading is not intended to produce a polished concert performance. The goals of sight-reading are to get to know a piece, to test our ability to hear what we see with our mind's ear, and to give a good impression of the contours, rhythms, pace, and general style of a passage. These goals cannot be met by stop-start reading. If you set out to give a good impression of the various elements of which the example is composed, admitting that even a good reading may involve occasional errors in details of one sort or another, you will make more progress and will develop greater facility and confidence than the reader who repeatedly stops and begins again.

Improvisation is a tool of sight-reading in that on-the-spot invention of the continuation of a figure or phrase representing an approximation of what is written is often far better than a dead stop.

Ideally one sight-reads all components of the passage: pitch, rhythm, dynamics, tempo, and so on. When the nature of a passage clearly precludes a comprehensive reading, attack the problematic aspect separately and then reread the passage in its complete form.

Try to avoid reference to the piano, or any other instrumental reinforcement. *Never* play what is to be sung except as a means for checking your accuracy *after* the passage has been sung. Use of the piano can result in a dependency that is hard to outgrow.

Preparation for Sight-Reading

Effective sightsinging demands taking several preparatory steps to be informed about the content and structure of a passage to be read. At the beginning of each section of music literature in this text, a number of simple preparatory steps are cited. These are to be routinely applied to the examples that follow. The preparatory checklist below contains several suggestions applicable to the performance of the music in Units One and Two. Additional procedures are given for the succeeding units.

CHECKLIST FOR SIGHTSINGING UNITS ONE AND TWO

Pitch

1. Note the general *lie* of the passage and its relation to your voice.
2. Determine the tonal center and scale basis; then relate the beginning and ending notes to the tonic. Refer to the key signature.
3. These examples are mainly conjunct; scan each example for contour, noting with care the kinds and placement of skips.
4. Note any altered notes and their relation to the tonality, for example, leading tone, decorative note, and so on.
5. Scan the phrase structure of each example and note the beginning and ending pitches of each phrase; note also their relation to tonic.

Rhythm

1. Note the meter signature and tempo.
2. Check for the various durations that occur in the passage. Where the rhythm is expected to pose difficulties in reading at sight, *intone the rhythm* before attempting to sing it.
3. Before beginning, establish the rhythmic level represented by the *shortest* recurring duration in the passage.
4. Observe recurring rhythmic patterns that unify the passage.

Interpretive Indications

Be aware of symbols denoting dynamic indications or articulation, especially where doing so may help you to show awareness of the character and style of the example.

A variety of interpretive symbols have been used in editing the music for this text. Some melodies are simply provided with broad phrase marks while others are marked with details of articulation, phrasing, dynamic nuance and the like, common to *instrumental* music. These are found especially in Units Two, Three, and Four.

Where no interpretive indications occur invent appropriate ones.

Based on the
Pre-Baroque Literature

part A
Introductory Materials Based on Traditional Melodies from Europe and the Americas

The materials in this part consist of melodies and duos from traditional folk music. The melodies are simple and singable. The purpose of their inclusion in this book is to provide an accessible starting point for everyone.

The melodies in this section will pose minimal difficulty for those who have had little or no vocal experience. They are largely conjunct, diatonic, and tonally stable, with no changes of key. Only simple meters occur in this section and as a rule syncopation has been avoided except in very rudimentary forms. Examples from this section could be used as warm-ups throughout the year.

Before singing each melody determine its tonal center and key. Sound the *tonic* pitch (using the piano or any available tool) and locate in your mind's ear the starting note of the example. Establish the tempo and meter by conducting a free measure or so and begin, singing the melody on the syllable *la*.

Note that a series of pitches appears under a slur following each melody. These represent capsule cues to the pitch-line of the preceding melody. If you are not able to negotiate successfully a given melodic example, refer to the cue that follows it; sing the cue and relate it to the pitches and contour of the melody it defines. Then, return to the complete tune and read it again. You will find that following this simple routine will help measurably with your performance of problematic examples.

Conducting

Conducting the meter while sightsinging helps to develop a beat consciousness that is essential to accurate rhythmic reading. Like any facet of musicianship, the ability to perform rhythm with a clearly defined feeling for meter can be developed and improved.

9

Learn the basic conductor's beat patterns given below and practice intoning rhythms while conducting the appropriate meter. When you have gained facility in coordinating reading and conducting, you will find that conducting the meter while sight-reading is a valuable tool for improving your overall performance of solo or ensemble music.

Conductor's Beat Patterns

Two-beat pattern ($\frac{2}{4}$, $\frac{6}{8}$, $\frac{6}{4}$, ¢)

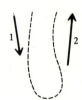

Three-beat pattern ($\frac{3}{4}$, $\frac{3}{2}$, $\frac{9}{8}$, and so on)

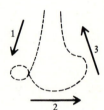

Four-beat pattern ($\frac{4}{4}$, $\frac{4}{2}$, $\frac{12}{8}$, and so on)

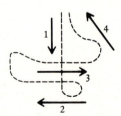

Five-beat pattern ($\frac{5}{4}$, $\frac{5}{8}$, and so on)

1. Division into 2 + 3

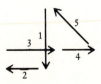
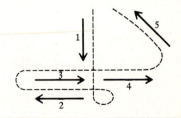

Preparatory Rhythmic Drills

Perform the following rhythms, conducting the meter while intoning the syllable
ta. Use a variety of tempi ranging from *adagio* to *presto.* You are urged to perform each exercise at several different tempi.

Traditional Melodies

1

Scottish

2

American

7   **Silesian**

10 **Hungarian**

Tempo giusto

11 **American**

Slow

think

12 **German**

Andante

13 **French**

Andante moderato

14   **English**

15   **Polish**

16   **French**

17　　　　　　　　　　　　　　　　　　　　　　　　　**English**

19 American

Slowly

20 U.S.

Moderato

21 American

Moderately

22   **English**

Slowly

23   **Sweden**

Andante

24   **German**

Andantino

25   **English**

Adagio

26   **French**

Andantino

27   **Polish**

Alla Polacca

28   **Alsatian**

Moderato

29   **Flemish**

Andante

30

Waltz

American

31

Boisterously

American

32

Moderately

33   **German**

Andante

34   **German**

Allegretto

35   **Swedish**

Slowly

36   **Spanish**

37   **Icelandic**

38   **Moderato**

39 U.S.

Slowly

40 U.S.

Slowly

41 Canadian

Moderately

42   **Polish**

43   **Silesian**

44   **German**

45   **German**

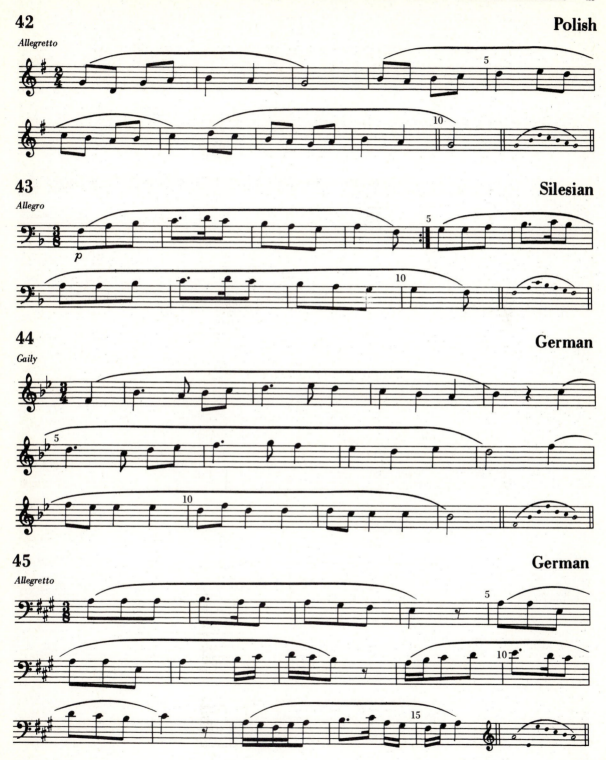

46

Slowly

47   **American**

Slowly

48   **American**

Quickly

49

English

Marcato

50

Francis Hopkinson

Slowly

51

William Billings

Adagietto

* This selection may be sung as a round for four voices, a new voice beginning the melody each time the first voice reaches an asterisk(*).

52

William Billings

Vigorously

53

American

Slowly

54

American

Slowly

55

William Billings

56

Italian

57　　　　　　　　　　　　　　　　　　　　　　　　　　**German**

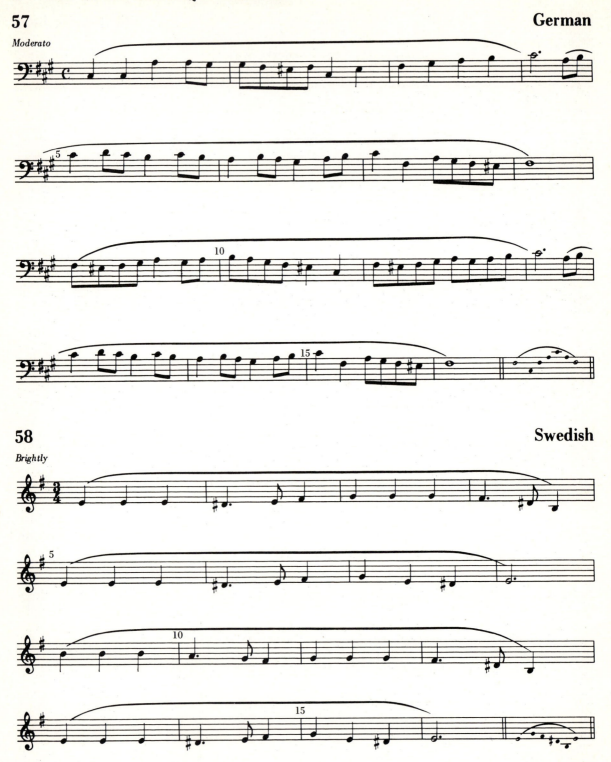

58　　　　　　　　　　　　　　　　　　　　　　　　　**Swedish**

59 German

Andante

60 English

Andantino

61 German

Lebhaft

62   German

63   Spanish

64   French

65 **German**

Andante

66 **American**

Spritely

67 **English**

Andante

68

English

Allegro

69

American

Allegretto

70 Scottish

71 German

72 German

Eight Duos on Traditional Tunes

73

English

75

William Billings

Slowly

76   **Swedish**

Brightly

77   **French**

Allegretto

78

Andante

Irish

79

Andante

Johann Sebastian Bach

80

Black Spiritual

80a

Duo ♩ = 112

80b

Variation ♩ = 90

81

Andantino

part B
Preparatory Exercises and Melodies from the Medieval and Renaissance Literature

The materials in this section are representative of Pre-Baroque music. Arranged in chronological order, these examples are generally diatonic, based on modal scales, nonmodulatory, and limited in the main to a range of about a tenth. The meters that appear are predominantly *simple duple* and *triple*. The alto clef is introduced in juxtaposition with examples in treble and bass clefs. *Syncopation* at various rhythmic levels occurs frequently. *Musica ficta* occurs largely in the form of leading tones.

In preparing to read these passages the student is urged to check the tonic (final pitch as a rule) of each example, as well as the prevailing *scale basis*. *Singing* the scale basis of a passage serves as a good preparation for performance.

For practice material particularly applicable to this part, students should refer to the Appendix Exercises 1–4. The instructor is encouraged to devise similar, additional practice materials as needed.

Preparatory Rhythmic Drill

Simple Triple Meter

* For comparison.

Preparatory Rhythmic Drill

Simple Duple Meter, Quadruple Meter

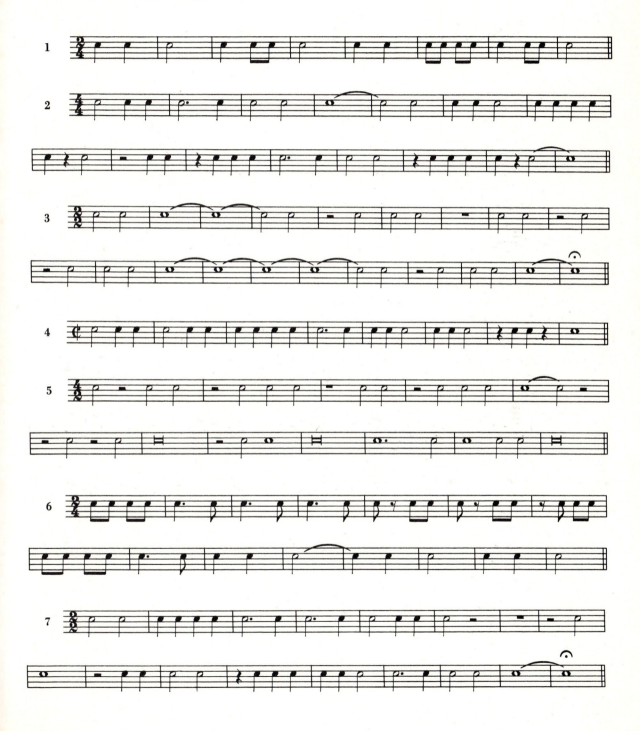

Preparatory Rhythmic Drill

Triple Meter with Syncopation

Preparatory Melodic Drill on Modal Scales

Dorian

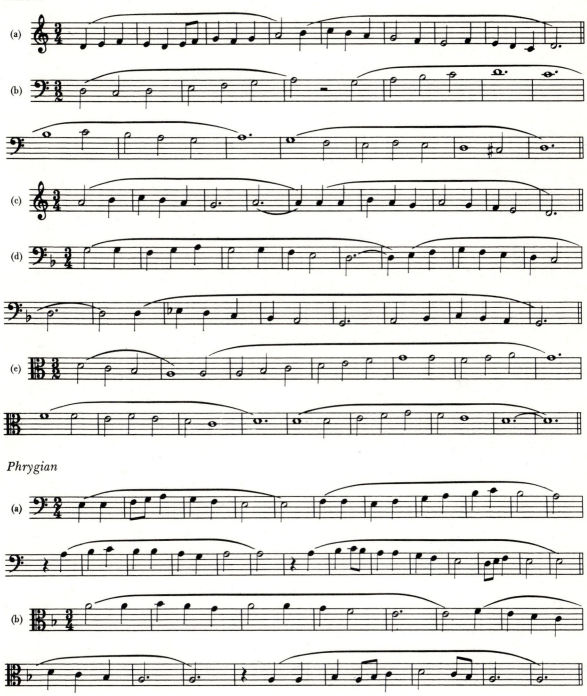

Phrygian

Lydian

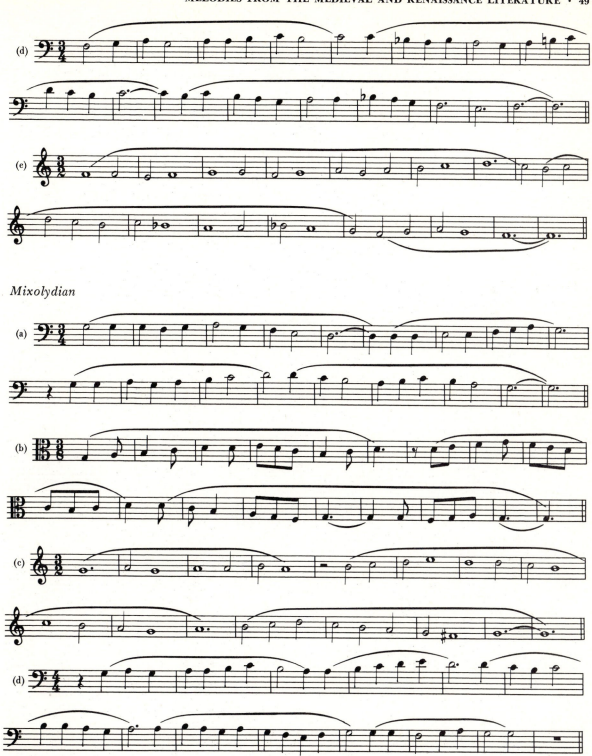

Mixolydian

Plainchant

The eight Gregorian chant melodies that follow illustrate the eight church modes in order. Although there is no simple, agreed-upon procedure for interpreting the rhythm of Gregorian chant, the time values suggested here may be assumed for reading purposes. Intone the examples using the suggested tempo for eighth notes suggested and sing the pitches on solfège syllables:

C = *do*
D = *re*
E = *mi*
F = *fa*
G = *sol*
A = *la*
B = *ti* (or *si*)*

82

Dorian

♪ = 132

Ky - ri - e * e - le - i - son. *iij.* Chri -

ste e - le - i - son. *iij.* Ky-ri - e e -

le - i - son. *ij.* Ky - ri - e * e - le - i - son.

* Use the same syllable for B-flat.

83

Hypodorian

♪ = 138

Ky - ri - e * e - le - i - son. Ky-

ri - e e - le - i - son. Ky - ri - e

e - le - i - son. Chri - ste e - le - i - son.

Chri - ste e - le - i - son. Chri - ste

e - li - i - son. Ky - ri - e e - le - i - son.

Ky - ri - e e - le - i - son. Ky - ri - e

e - le - i - son.

* Caesura.

84

Phrygian

(♪ = 132)

Ký - ri - e   *   e - lé - i -

son. *iij.* Chrí - ste

e - lé - i - son. *iij.* Ký - ri - e

e - lé - i - son. *iij.* Ký - ri - e   *

**   e - lé - i - son.

85

Hypophrygian

(♪ = 132)

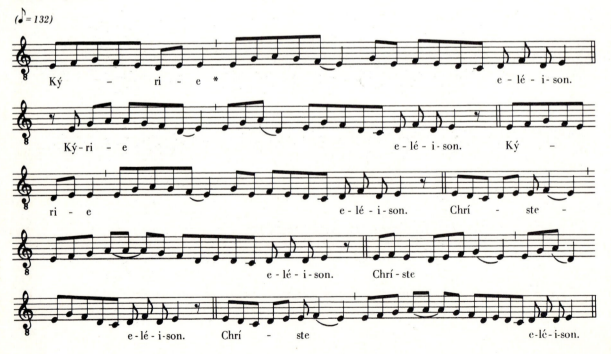

Ký - ri - e *   e - lé - i - son.

Ký - ri - e   e - lé - i - son.   Ký -

ri - e   e - lé - i - son.   Chrí - ste -

e - lé - i - son.   Chrí - ste

e - lé - i - son.   Chrí - ste   e - lé - i - son.

86
Lydian

(♩= 138)

Ký - ri - e   *   e - lé - i - son. *iij.*

Chrí - ste   e - lé - i - son.   *iij.*

Ký - ri - e   e - lé - i - son.   *iij.*

Ký - ri - e   *   **e - lé - i - son.

87
Hypolydian

(M.M. ♩= 144.)

Ký - ri - e   * e - lé - i - son.   *iij.*

Chrí - ste   e - lé - i - son.   *iij.*

Ký - ri - e   e - lé - i - son.   *iij.*

Ký - ri - e   *   **   e - lé - i - son.

88

Mixolydian

(M.M. ♪ = 144.)

Gló - ri - a in ex - cél - sis Dé - o.

Et in tér - ra pax ho - mí - ni - bus bó - nae vo - lun - ta - tis.

Lau - dá - mus te. Be - ne - dí - ci - mus te.

A - do - rá - mus te. Glo - ri - fi - cá - mus te.

Grá - ti - as á - gim - us tí - bi prop - ter má - gnam gló - ri - am tú - am.

89

Hypomixolydian

(M.M. ♪ = 138.)

Ký - ri - e *e - lé - i - son. iij.

Chrí - ste e - lé - i - son. iij.

Ký - ri - e *e - lé - i - son. iij.

90   **Bernart de Ventadorn**

91   **Anon.**

92   **Adam de la Halle**

93

Moderato

Thibaut de Navarre

94

Slowly

Anon.

95

Devoutly

Walther von der Vogelweide

96

Anon. 13th c.

97

Anon.

Ars Nova and Renaissance Melodies, 1300–1600

98

Guillaume de Machaut

99

Francesco Landini

100

Guillaume de Machaut

101

Guillaume de Machaut

102

Guillaume de Machaut

103

Guillaume de Machaut

104

Guillaume de Machaut

105

Guillaume Dufay

106

Guillaume Dufay

*Instrumental interlude deleted.

107

Guillaume Dufay

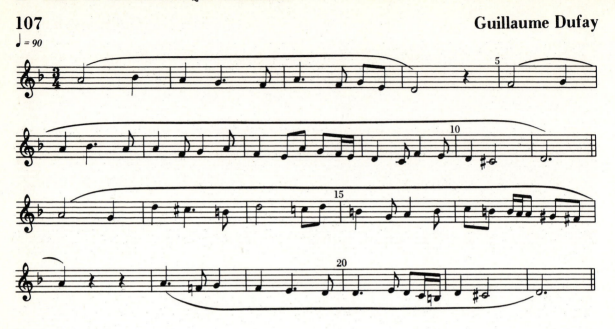

108

Gillis Binchois

109   **Gillis Binchois**

110   **Johannes Ockeghem**

111   Johannes Ockeghem

112   Johannes Ockeghem

113

Johannes Ockeghem

114

Johannes Ockeghem

115

Heinrich Isaac

116

Josquin des Prez

117

Jacob Obrecht

118   Josquin des Prez

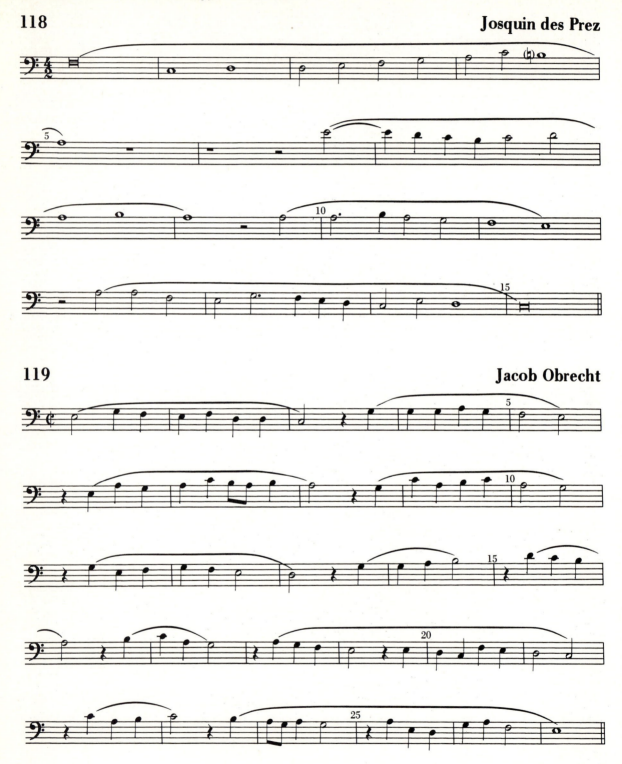

119   Jacob Obrecht

120

Bartolomeo Tromboncino

121

Bartolomeo Tromboncino

122

Anon.

123

Anon.

124 Vincent Faugues

125 Johannes Regis

126 Anon.

127

Johannes Ockeghem

128

Johannes Ockeghem

129

Anon.

Duos and Vocal Ensembles
from the
Medieval and Renaissance Literature

Accurate performance of these duos is more likely to result if each performer tries to be aware of both musical lines. Each line should be heard as a melody that is forming harmonic and rhythmic relations with another voice. The reader should be aware, for example, of passages in which both parts move in rhythmic alignment, and of those marked by rhythmic independence. Once again, reading ahead is essential to note such important points in the tonal structure as unisons, octaves or fifths, especially at beginning, ending and climactic points. Perhaps the most essential rule of thumb for effective ensemble reading involves *listening to each other*.

130

Anon. 13th c.

131

Guillaume de Machaut

132

Guillaume de Machaut

133

Guillaume de Machaut

134

John Dunstable

135

Guillaume Dufay

136

Guillaume Dufay

137

Guillaume Dufay

*Include all such altered notes.

138

Guillaume Dufay

*Include all such altered notes.

139

Guillaume Dufay

140

Guillaume Dufay

* This optional 2-measure instrumental ostinato may be repeated throughout.

141

Gilles Binchois

142

Anon.

143

Anon.

144

Antoine Busnois

145

Gilles Binchois

146

Gilles Binchois

147

Johannes Ockeghem

San - - - - - - - -

San - - - - - -

- - - - ctus, San -

ctus, San - - - -

- ctus, San - - -

- ctus, San - - -

- - - - - ctus.

- - - - ctus.

148

Johannes Ockeghem

149

Johannes Ockeghem

150

Josquin des Prez

151

Josquin des Prez

152

Josquin des Prez

Sanc - tus, sanc - tus, sanc - - -

Sanc - tus, sanc - tus, sanc - - -

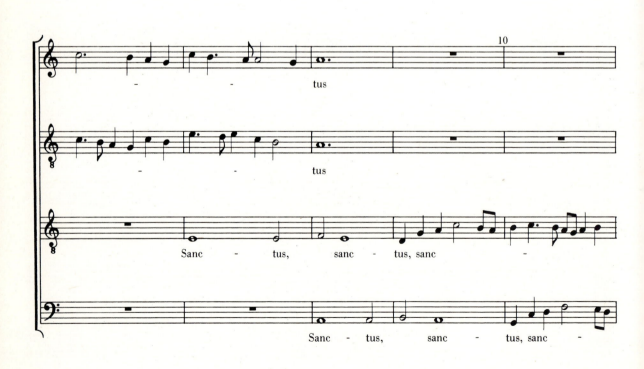

- - tus

- - tus

Sanc - tus, sanc - tus, sanc -

Sanc - tus, sanc - tus, sanc -

Do - mi-nus De - us Sa - ba - oth,

Do - mi-nus De - us Sa - ba-oth, Sa -

- tus Do - mi-nus De - - us

- tus Do - mi-nus De - us Sa -

Sa - ba - oth, Sa-ba - oth, Sa-ba - oth.

- - ba - oth, Sa-ba - oth, Sa-ba - oth.

Sa - ba - oth, Sa-ba - oth.

- - ba - oth, Sa-ba - oth.

153

Josquin des Prez

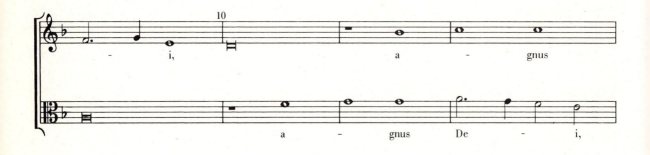

qui tol - - lis pec - ca -

- lis pec - ca -

- - - ta mun - -

- - ta mun - di, mun -

di, mun - di, mi - se - re -

- di, mi - se - re - -

- - - re no - bis.

- - re no - - bis.

154

Josquin des Prez

155

Josquin des Prez

156   **Johannes Lupus Hellinck**

157

Jacob Obrecht

158

Jacob Obrecht

159

Heinrich Isaac

160

Claude de Sermisy

Pit - y on me for all I must en - dure

Pit - y on me for all I must en - dure

To serve you

To serve you though I want it

though I want it not

not, I want it not,

For Love can make you love as I

For Love can make you love as I

do; And make you pay

do; And make you pay the price for

the price for your past cru - - - el - ty, cru

your past cru - - - el - ty, cru

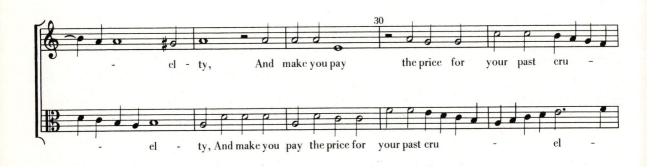

- el - ty, And make you pay the price for your past cru - el -

- el - ty, And make you pay the price for your past cru - el -

- - - el - ty ____ the price.

ty, And make you pay ____ the price.

161   Giovanni da Palestrina

162

Bartolomeo Tromboncino

Accompaniment*

* Performance by voice and guitar suggested.

163   **Roland de Lassus**

Car - mi - na chro - ma - ti -

Car - mi - na chro - ma - ti -

Car - mi - na...

Car - mi - na...

co quae au - dis mo - du - la - ta te - no -

re, Haec sunt il - la qui - bus

no - strae o - lim ar - ca - na sa - lu -

tis Bis se - nae in - tre - pi - do ce - ci - ne runt, ce - ci - ne -

runt o - re si - byl - lae.

164

Jacob Arcadelt

165

Carlo Gesualdo

166

Antonio de Cabezón

167

Johann Walther

168

Marco Cara

Io non com - pro piu spe - ran - za Che gli e fal -

Accompaniment*

sa mer can - ci - a. A dar sol at - ten - do vi - a

Quel la po - ca che m'a - van - za. Io non com - pro piu spe -

* Performance by voice and guitar suggested.

ran - za   Che gli e fal - sa   mer - can - ci - a,   che gli e

fal - sa   mer - can - ci   -   -   -   -   -

a.

169

Jacob Arcadelt

Io mi ri - voi - go in - die - tro, io mi ri -

Io mi ri - voi - go in - die - tro, io mi ri -

Io mi ri - voi - go in - die -

Io mi ri - voi - go in - die -

voi - go in - die - tro a cia - scun pas - so Col

voi - go in - die - tro a cia - scun pas - so Col

tro a cia - scun pas so, a cia - scun pas - so Col cor - po

tro a cia - scun pas - so, a cia - scun pas - so Col

170

Thomas Weelkes

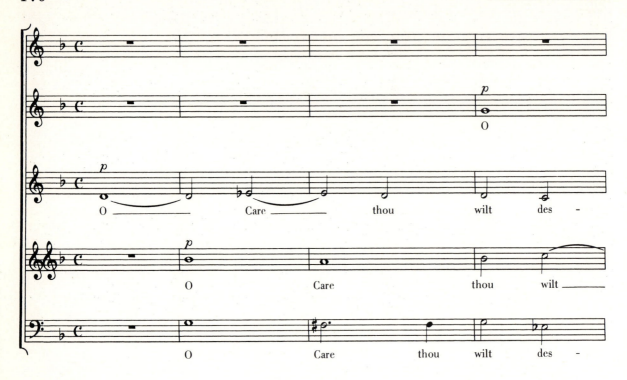

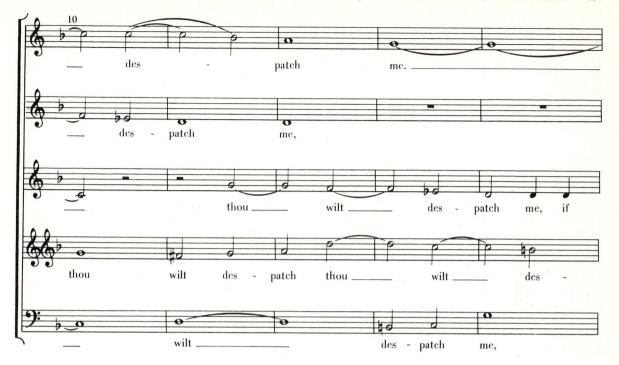

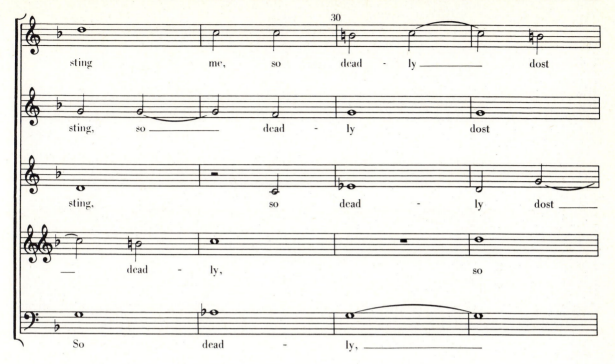

Unit Two

Based on the Baroque, Viennese-Classical, and Romantic Literature

Preparatory Exercises and Melodies from the Seventeenth-, Eighteenth-, and Nineteenth-Century Literature

This part introduces compound meter, key change, the tenor clef, and increasingly varied forms of syncopation and beat division/subdivision. Both vocal and instrumental examples are provided.

PART D CONTAINS:

Sight-Reading and Formal Organization
Melodic Incipits
Chorales: Johann Sebastian Bach
Preparatory Rhythmic Exercises
Melodies for Sightsinging: From Scheidt to Fauré

Exercises in the Appendix most pertinent to Part D: Nos. 1 to 10.

Sight-Reading and Formal Organization

The ability to read at sight can be enhanced by an awareness of the processes that help shape and unify a melodic line. This is particularly true when applied to the level of phrase-to-phrase or pattern-to-pattern relationships. The medodic excerpts that follow are typical of most tonal music in making use of a variety of organizing devices, such as:

melodic phrase repetition (no. 7);
modified melodic phrase repetition (no. 4);
exact rhythmic phrase repetition (no. 6);
sequence (no. 8);
extended sequence (no. 20);
rhythmically parallel periods (no. 13).

In preparation for reading the melodic excerpts that follow, scan each example, noting these and other devices as they occur. Then sing the examples on *la* or *ta*.

Franz Schubert

Andante un poco mosso

(6)

Franz Schubert

Ziemlich langsam

(7)

Alessandro Scarlatti

Allegretto grazioso, leggiero

(8)

Niccolò Piccinni

Allegro

(9)

Domenico Scarlatti

Johann Sebastian Bach

Giacomo Meyerbeer

Joseph Haydn

Franz Schubert

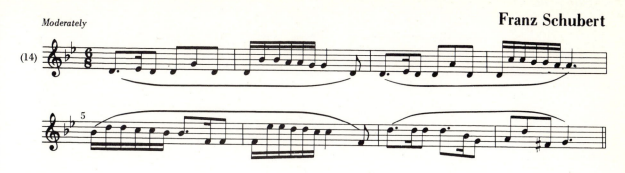

Gustav Mahler

Wolfgang Amadeus Mozart

Georg Philipp Telemann

Melodic Incipits

The fifteen passages that follow are representative of eighteenth- and nineteenth-century melody. Test your ability to give a good approximation of these characteristic, short, opening passages of one or two phrases by sounding the first note, establishing the meter and tempo, and singing each passage, using an appropriate form of vocalization. A sample vocalization such as might be applied to melody no. 8 is given below.

Chorales

THESE CHORALES MAY BE USED IN A NUMBER OF WAYS:

1. as class warm-ups;
2. as duos for soprano and bass or any other pair or voices;
3. playing one or more parts and singing another part;
4. as exercises in vertical chord singing;
5. as linear pitch drills for any single voice.

Johann Sebastian Bach

Break forth, O love - ly morn - ing light, There by the heav - ens
Ye shep - herd folk, do not take fright Be - cause of an - gels'

light - ing. That this so weak and low - ly child Will
cit - ing

be our hope and Sav - ior mild, Will bonds of Sa - tan

Johann Sebastian Bach

sev - er, And bring us peace for - ev - er.

It is e - nough! Lord, by Thy wise de - cree

I gird me to de - part. My Je - sus comes! Fare - well, O

world, to thee; I seek my heav'n - ly home. In peace I

trav - el sure - ly on - ward; Be - hind is earth - ly grief and

Johann Sebastian Bach

Johann Sebastian Bach

Johann Sebastian Bach

(e)

When   I   too   am   de - part - ing, Then   part   Thou   not   from   me:
On   death's lone   jour - ney   start - ing, My   soul   will   feel   for   Thee.

When   near   my   end   I   lan - guish, All   oth - er   com - fort   vain,

Then   draw   me   out   of   an - guish, Through Thy vic - to - rious   pain.

Johann Sebastian Bach

With joy - ful heart we now sur - round The hal - lowed East - er ta - ble,
The Word of Grace doth now con - found The leav - en old, un - sta - ble.

Christ a - lone will be our food, For hun - gry souls the live - li - hood:

In faith none else is ten - a - ble. Al - le - lu - ia!
Al - le - lu - ia!
Al - le - lu - ia!

Preparatory Rhythmic Exercises

Many of the rhythmic patterns common to music of the eighteenth and nineteenth centuries are found in the exercises presented here and in the rhythmic duos in Part E. These rhythms are to be intoned on a neutral syllable such as *la* or *ta*.

Conducting or tapping the *meter* while intoning the rhythm is recommended. Tapping the *rhythm* should be avoided, however, since this fails to differentiate the length of one note from another.*

Use a variety of tempi for rhythmic reading. Covering the measure being performed with your hand or a card insures better reading ahead. Try to take in each measure as a unit to be read as a whole, rather than reading successive, separate notes.

Compound meter is introduced in the examples that follow. In compound time the beat unit is divided by three, in contrast to the division by two found in simple meters. The most commonly used beat units in compound time and their usual beat divisions and subdivisions are pictured below. Keep in mind that the beat in compound time is a dotted note, as shown below:

BEAT   BEAT DIVISION   BEAT SUBDIVISION

* It is impossible to *sustain* a tap.

(3)

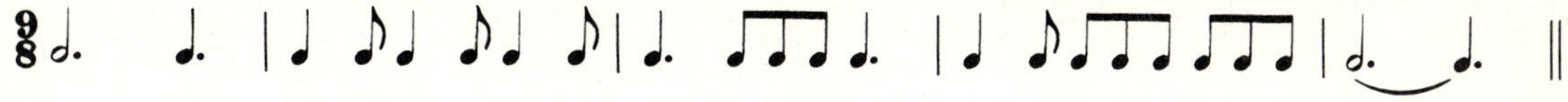

(4)

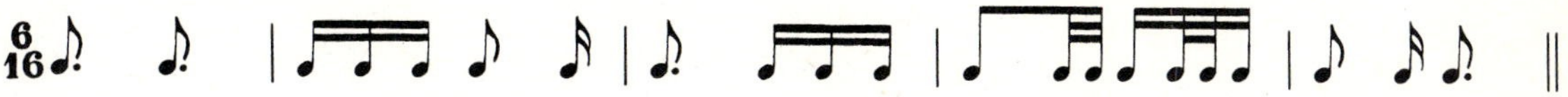

(5)

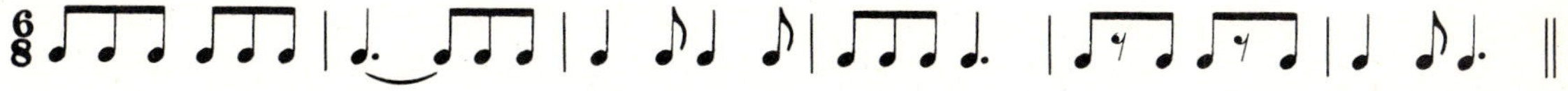

(6)

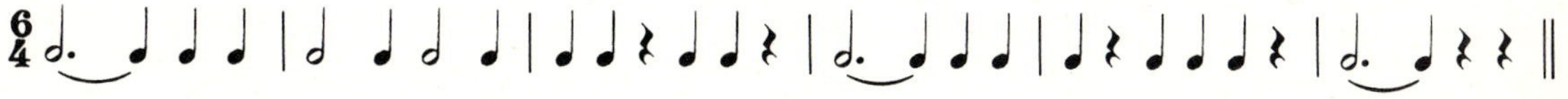

(7)

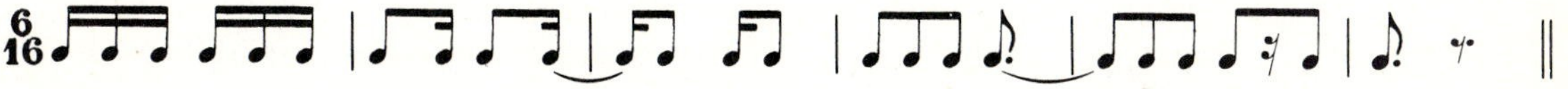

(8)

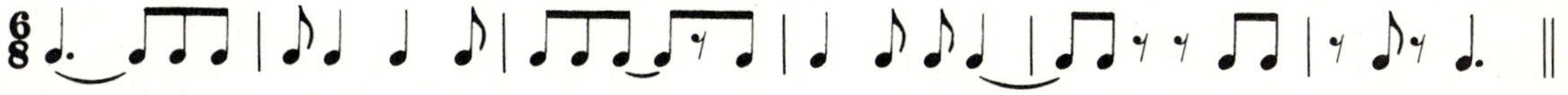

(9)

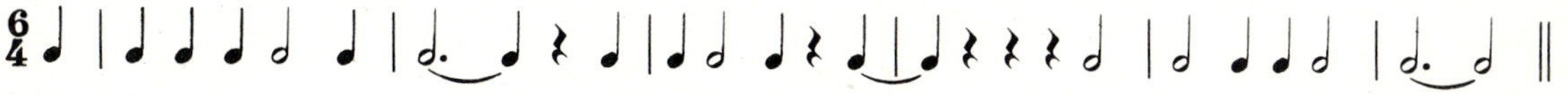

(10)

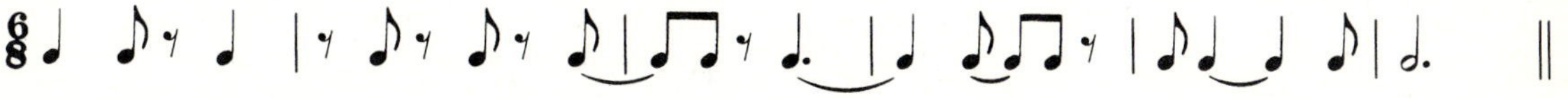

(11) [musical notation]

(12) [musical notation]

(13) [musical notation]

(14) [musical notation]

(15) [musical notation]

Syncopated Patterns in Simple and Compound Meters

These preparatory rhythmic exercises present a considerable variety of beat division and syncopation. Observe the dynamic markings in performance, and use a variety of tempi. Be sure that the meter and tempo are established for at least one measure before beginning to intone on *ta*. It is also important to establish in your mind's ear the length of the *shortest* note duration in a given pattern before beginning to intone. For example, the eighth notes of no. 1 must be pre-heard if their performance in context is to be accurate. Similarly, the thirty-second notes of no. 7 must be *already under way* in the performer's mind before beginning. Intone thirty-second notes for a "free measure" before beginning. Then:

1. establish the quarter-note beat level (2);
$$4$$
2. maintain the beat by tapping, and intone 32nds against the beat;

3. keep the 32nds *active* in your mind's ear and begin the exercise.

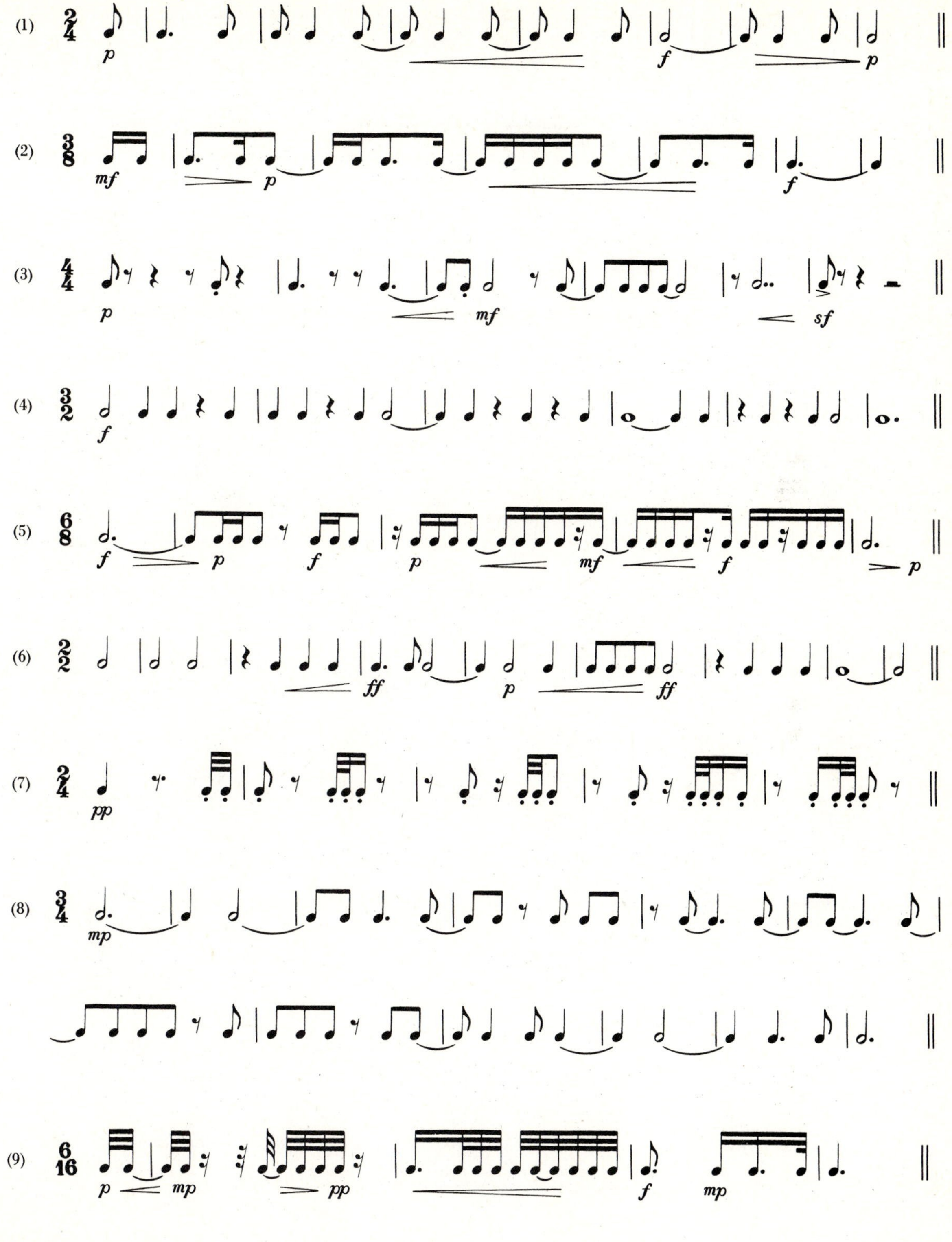
(1)
(2)
(3)
(4)
(5)
(6)
(7)
(8)
(9)

(10)

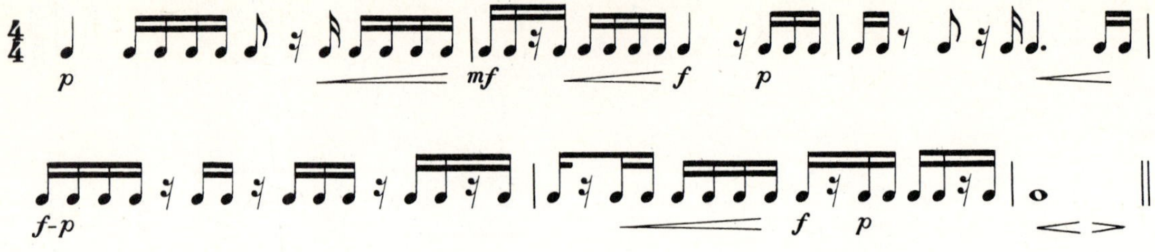

(11)

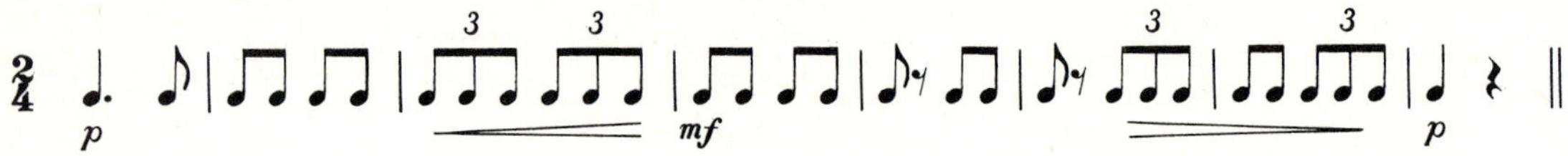

(12)

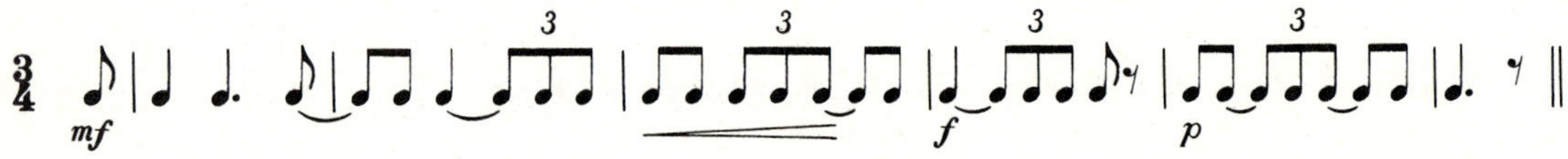

(13)

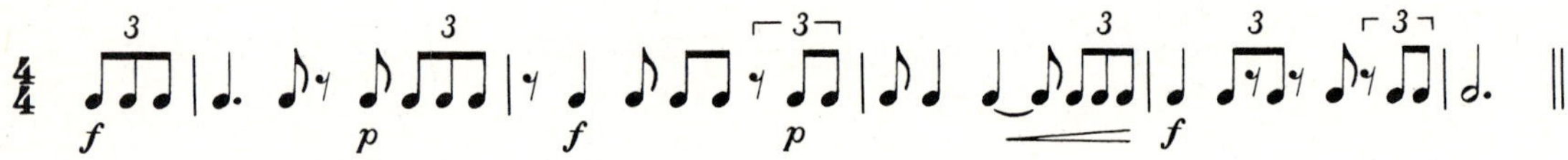

(14)

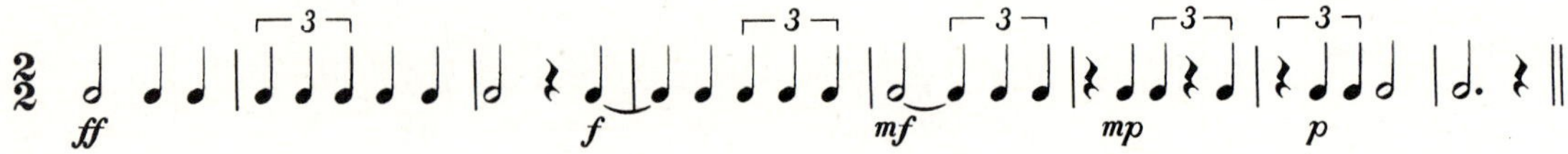

(15)

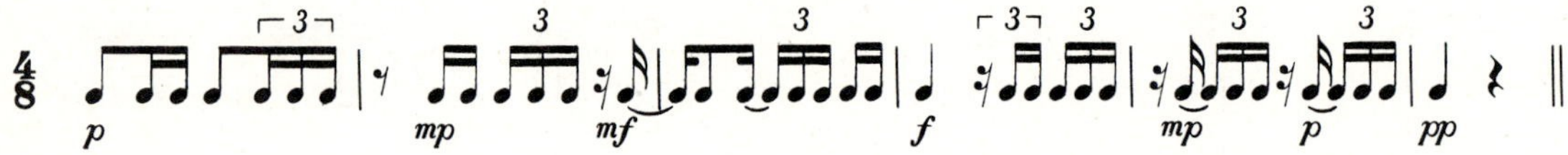

(16)

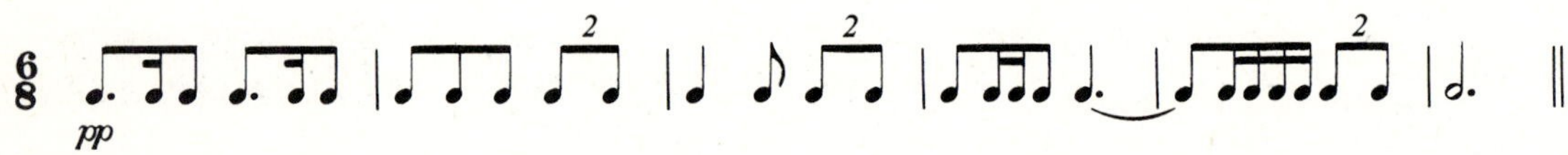

(17)

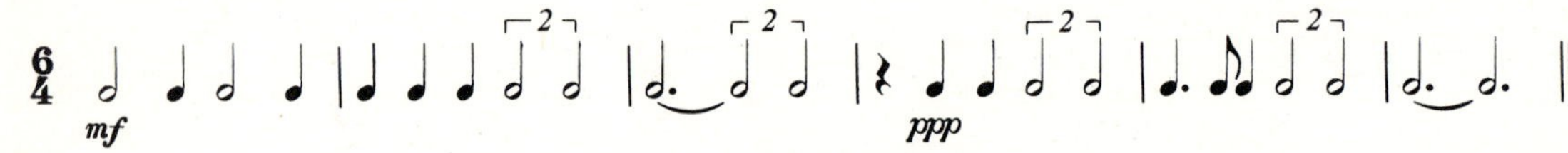

(18)

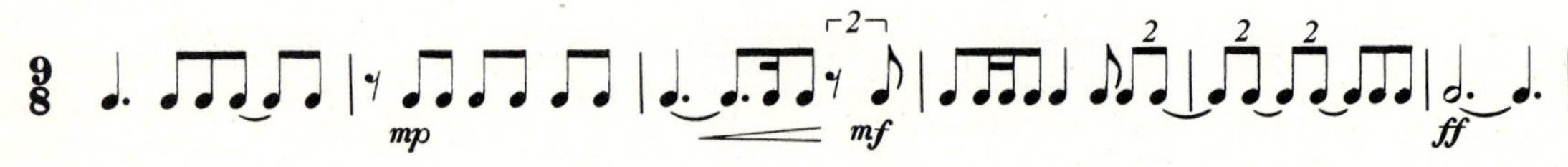

(19)

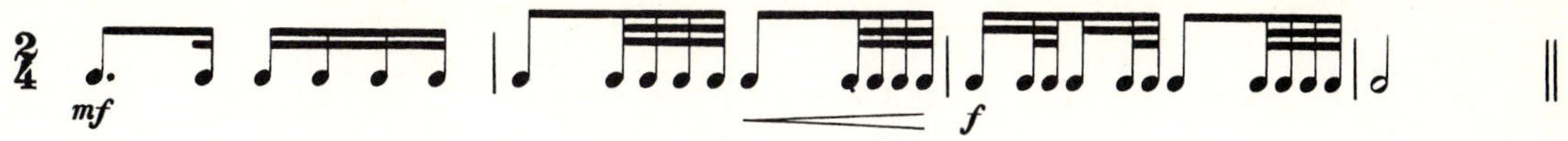

(20)

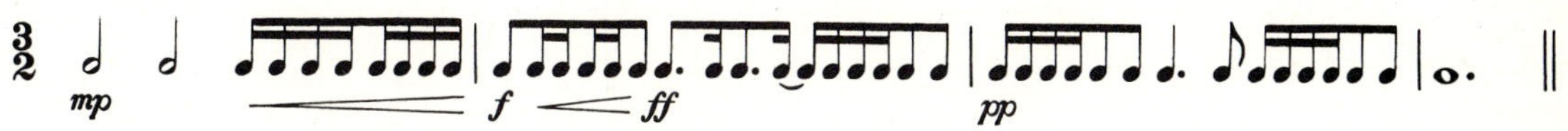

(21)

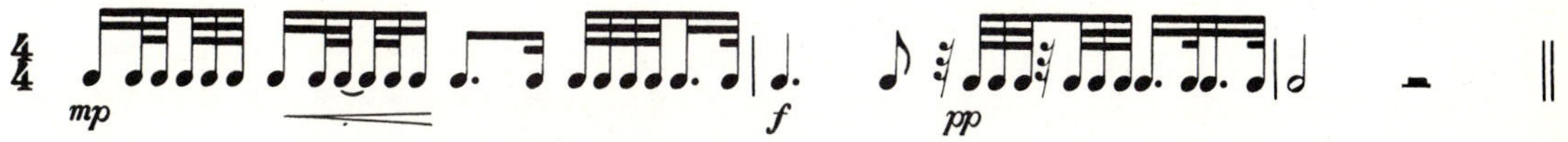

(22)

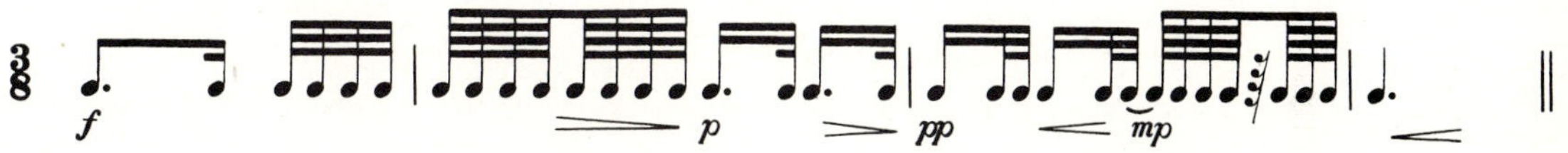

(23)

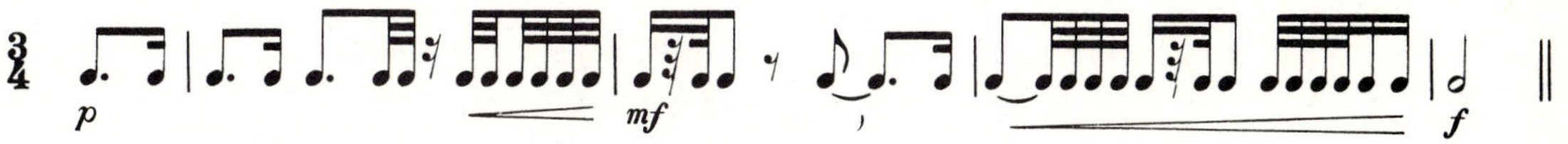

(24)

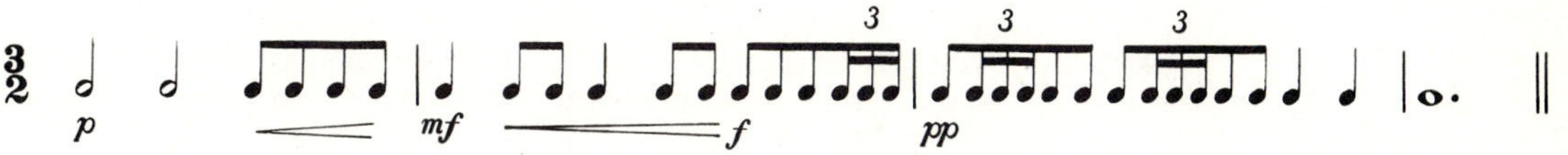

(25)

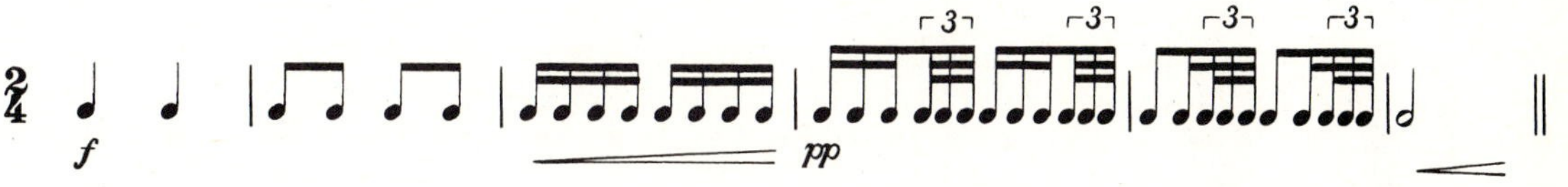

(26)

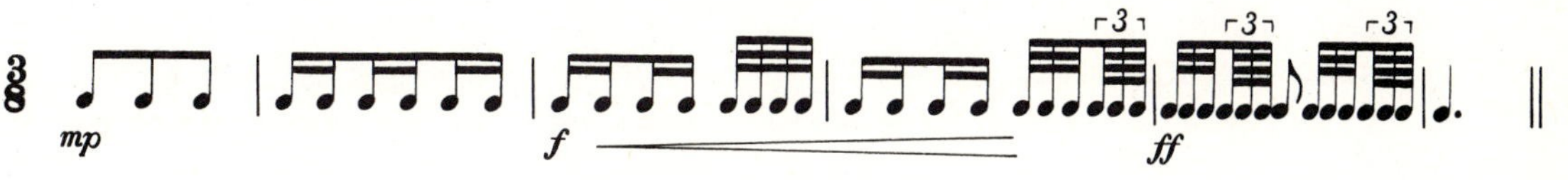

(27)

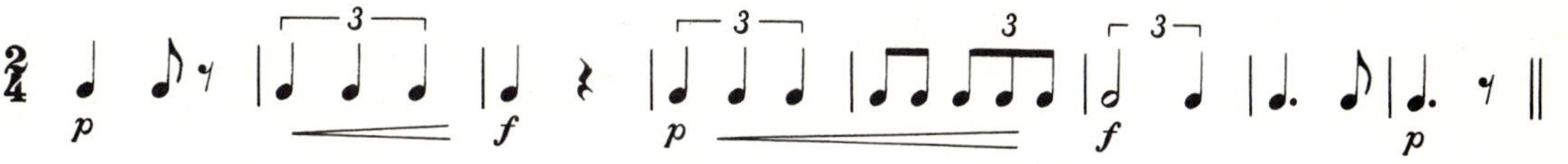

(28)

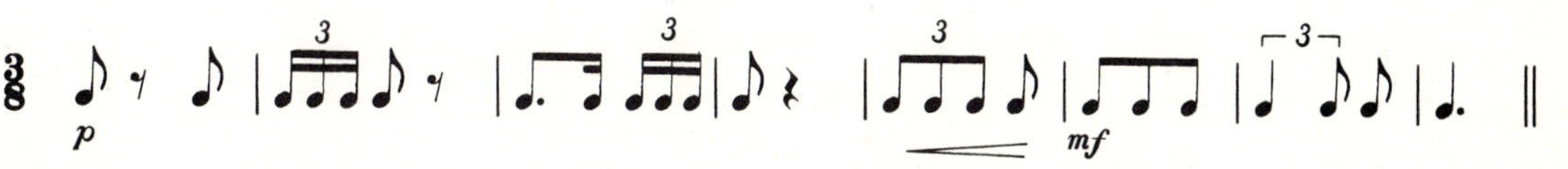

(29)
f p f pp
(30)
ff
(31)
pp p ppp pp
(32)
f p f
(33)
p mp f
(34)
f p f p pp
(35)
ff pp ff
(36)
ppp p
(37)
p mf f
p mf

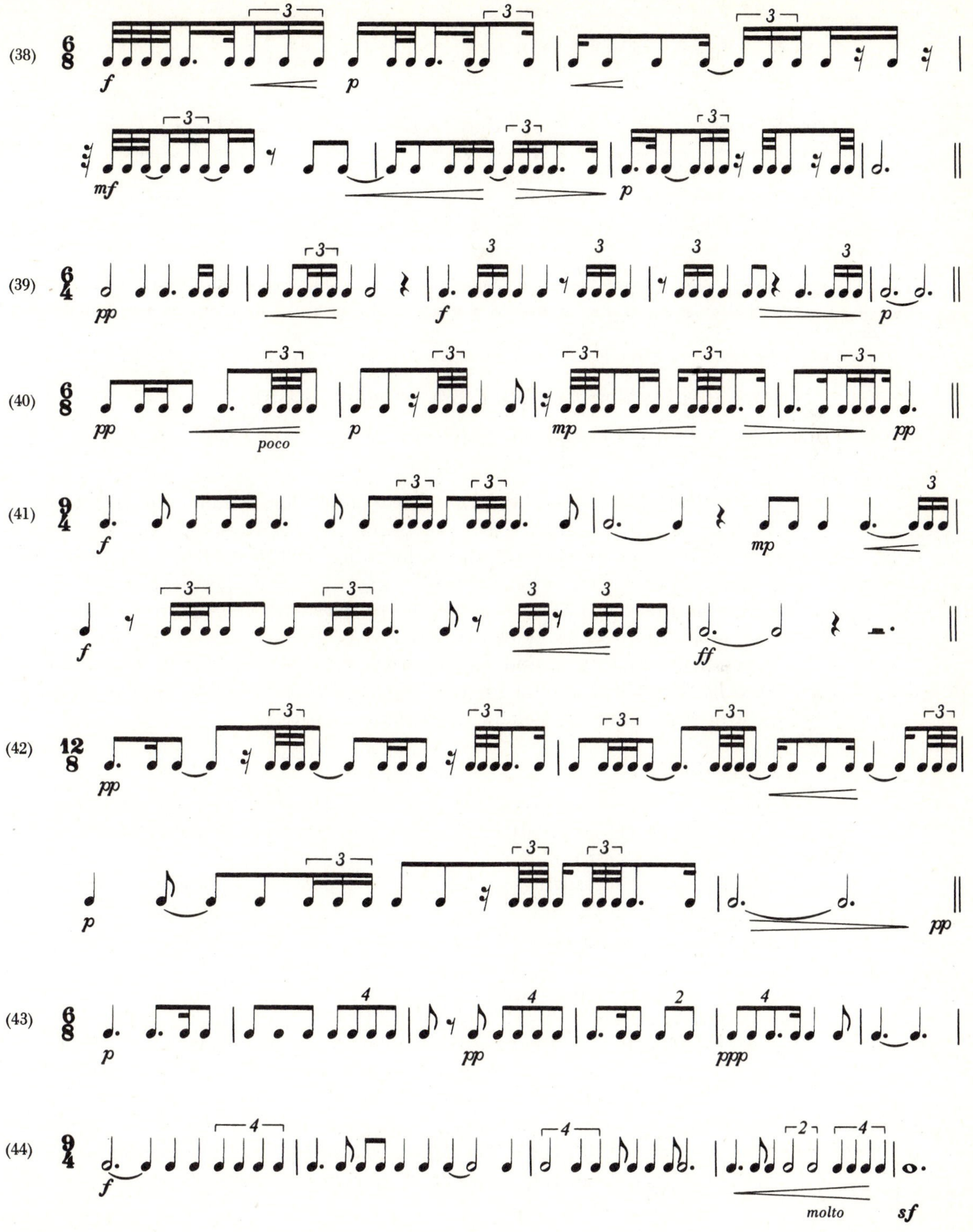
(38)
(39)
(40)
poco
(41)
(42)
(43)
(44)
molto
sf

Melodies for Sightsinging: From Scheidt to Fauré

Suggestions for reading

These melodies are selected from the literature that includes the work of Bach, Haydn, Mozart, Beethoven, Schubert, and Brahms, together with works by a number of other composers of the period from 1600 to 1900. This body of music is unique in revealing certain stylistic norms that set it apart from music written before or after the 300-year span of the period of common practice. The reader can approach melodies of this period with a number of expectations that will generally be realized in study or performance of the music itself. The following checklist takes into account such expectations, and should be applied systematically in preparation for melodic sight-reading.

CHECKLIST

1. Note the meter and tempo; then observe the various note durations that occur as well as recurring rhythmic *patterns*, syncopations, and changes of rhythmic density.
2. Check for organizing devices such as repetition or sequence, cited at the beginning of this unit.
3. Be aware of the contour of each melody; note the high and low points, and relate them to the key of the melody.
4. Scan the melodic phrase structure, noting the relation of *cadence* notes to the tonality.
5. Establish in your mind's ear the notes of the tonic triad, scale degrees 1, 3, 5 (and 8). These stable notes in a key provide a framework for melodic detail while acting as reference pitches.
6. Scan each melody for *accidentals* foreign to the key of the melody; determine the role of accidentals as decorative (passing or neighboring tones, for example), structural (as members of implied chords, or as members of a new key).

171

Samuel Scheidt

Maestro

172

Friedrich Wilhelm Zachau

Allegretto

173

Antonio Caldara

Canon for 3 voices*

174

Henry Purcell

Allegro moderato

*The second voice begins when the first voice reaches the number 2; the third voice begins when the second voice reaches the number 2.

175

Johann Sebastian Bach

176

George Frederick Handel

177

Alessandro Scarlatti

Largo

178

Benedetto Marcello

Adagio

poco rit.

179

Johann Sebastian Bach

180

Johann Sebastian Bach

Allegro

181

Johann Sebastian Bach

Polacca

182

Johann Sebastian Bach

Allegro

183

Johann Sebastian Bach

Allegro

184

Johann Sebastian Bach

185

Johann Sebastian Bach

Andante

186
Adagio

Johann Sebastian Bach

187
Grave

Johann Sebastian Bach

188

Johann Sebastian Bach

Andante

189

Johann Sebastian Bach

Largo pathetico

190

Johann Sebastian Bach

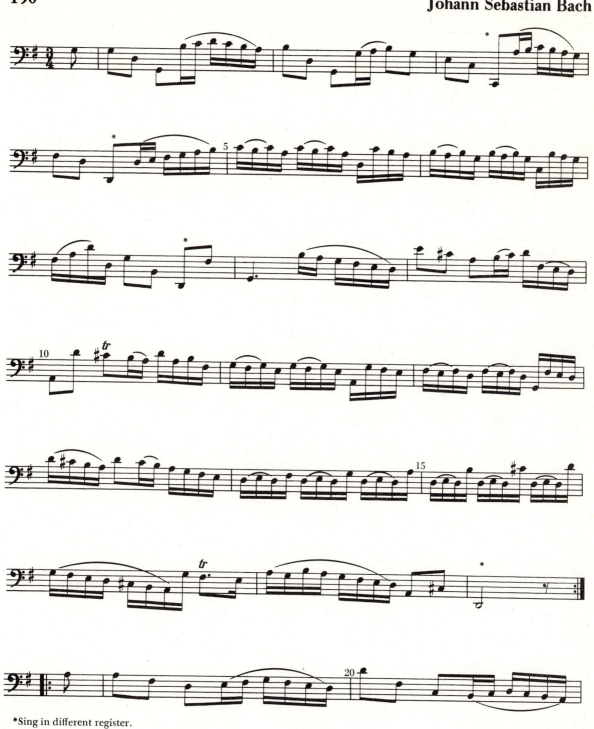

*Sing in different register.

*Sing in different register.

191

Adagio

Johann Sebastian Bach

D.C. al Fine

192

Johann Sebastian Bach

193

Johann Sebastian Bach

Allegro

194

George Frederick Handel

195

George Frederick Handel

196

George Frederick Handel

197

George Frederick Handel

Largo

198

Wolfgang Amadeus Mozart

Adagio non troppo

199

Wolfgang Amadeus Mozart

200

Allegro

Wolfgang Amadeus Mozart

201

Wolfgang Amadeus Mozart

202

Wolfgang Amadeus Mozart

Allegro

203
Allegretto

Wolfgang Amadeus Mozart

204
Presto

Wolfgang Amadeus Mozart

207

Wolfgang Amadeus Mozart

Allegro

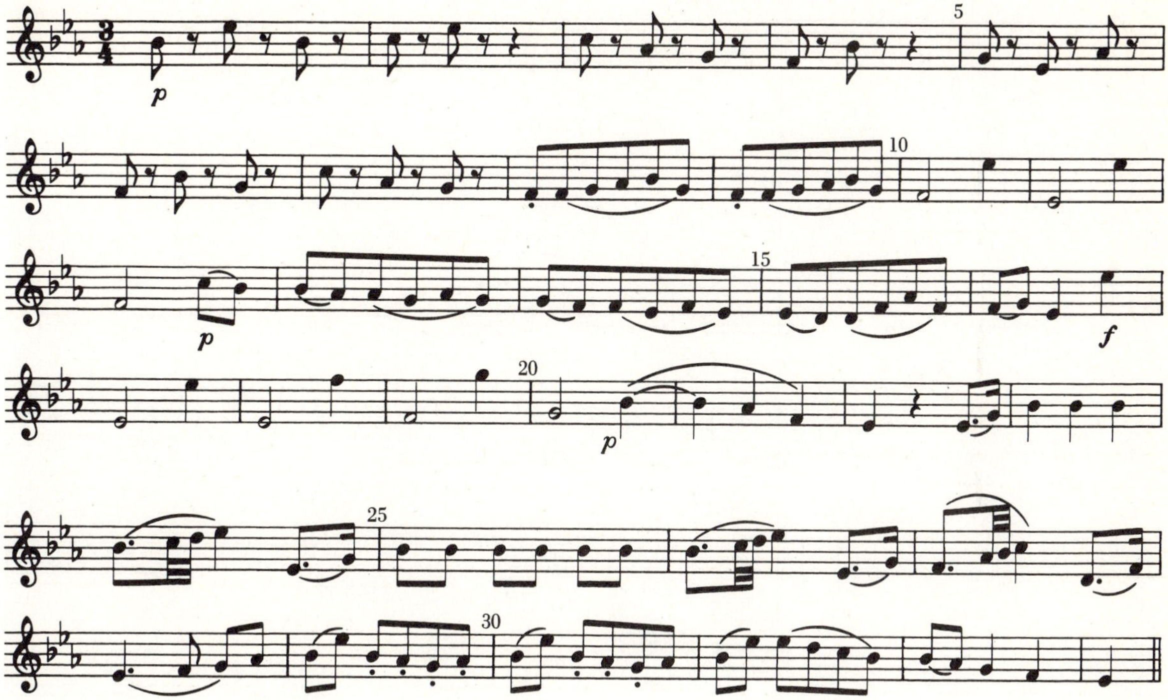

208

Wolfgang Amadeus Mozart

Con moto

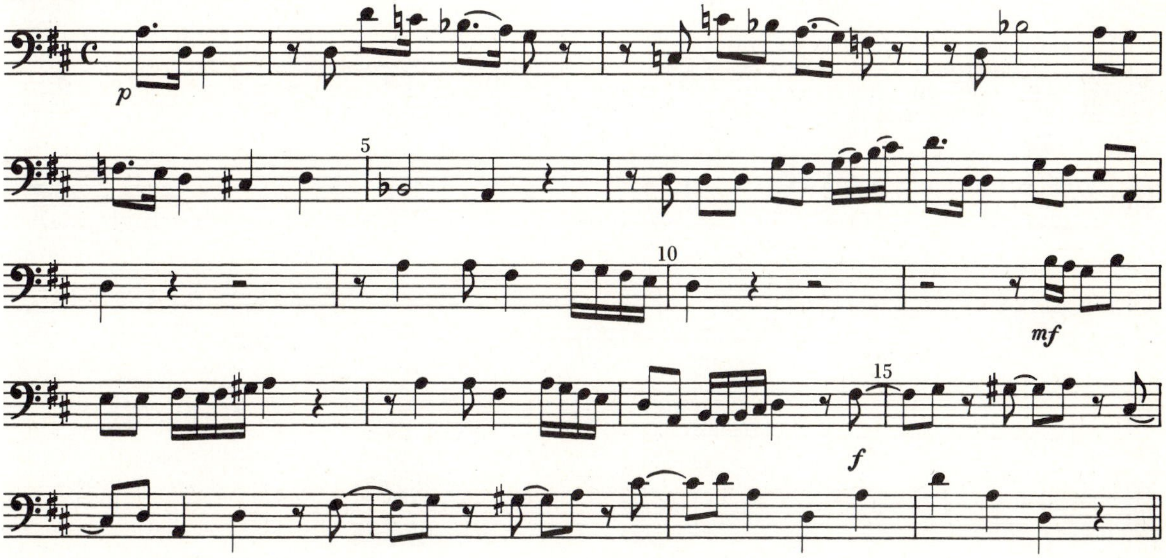

209

Joseph Haydn

211

Joseph Haydn

212

Joseph Haydn

213

Joseph Haydn

214

Joseph Haydn

215

Moderato cantible

Joseph Haydn

216

Allegretto

Joseph Haydn

217

Joseph Haydn

Allegro ma non troppo

218

Ludwig van Beethoven

Adagio cantabile

219

Andante con variazoni

Ludwig van Beethoven

220

Ludwig van Beethoven

221   **Ludwig van Beethoven**

Allegro molto

222   **Ludwig van Beethoven**

Andante

223   Ludwig van Beethoven

224   Ludwig van Beethoven

225   Ludwig van Beethoven

*The second voice begins when the first voice reaches the number 2; the third voice begins when the second voice reaches the number 2.

226
Ludwig van Beethoven

230

Franz Schubert

Massig

231

Franz Schubert

Etwas geschwind

232

Franz Schubert

Massig geschwind

233

Franz Schubert

Langsam

236   **Franz Schubert**
Allegro

237   **Franz Schubert**
Mässig

238

Franz Schubert

239

Franz Schubert

240

Felix Mendelssohn

Presto

241

Felix Mendelssohn

Adagio

245

♩ = 72

Felix Mendelssohn

246

Animato

Frédéric Chopin

247

Frédéric Chopin

248

Robert Schumann

249

Allegro

Robert Schumann

250

Adagio

Robert Schumann

251

Andante cantabile

Robert Schumann

252

Robert Schumann

Allegro

253

Hector Berlioz

Adagio un poco lento e dolce assai

254

Georges Bizet

255

Modest Mussorgsky

256

Fierlich

Richard Wagner

257   Richard Wagner

Sempre molto tranquillo

258   Robert Franz

Andantino

259
Allegro (♩. = 1 beat)

Johannes Brahms

260
Gehend

Johannes Brahms

261
Adagio

Johannes Brahms

262   Johannes Brahms

Poco allegretto

263   Johannes Brahms

Allegro non troppo

264

Johannes Brahms

265

Johannes Brahms

268

Munter, mit freiem Vortrag

Johannes Brahms

269

Johannes Brahms

Allegretto grazioso

270

Johannes Brahms

Adagio

271

Andante

Anton Bruckner

272

Vivo

Ernest Chausson

273

Gustav Mahler

274

Gemachlich

Gustav Mahler

275

Schnell und wild

Gustav Mahler

276

Gustav Mahler

277

Vincent d'Indy

Moderement lent

278

Gabriel Fauré

Andante quasi allegretto

279

part E

Vocal Duos Adapted from the Seventeenth-, Eighteenth-, and Nineteenth-Century Literature

These duos are selected from the ensemble repertoire from ca. 1600 to 1900, and include a variety of vocal, keyboard, and instrumental genres. The selections have been adapted to be sung in two parts, or sung and played by one person.

Scan each duo *before* beginning to perform and take into account apparent changes of tonality, chromaticism, and rhythmic levels. Note also any clef changes* that are introduced.

PART E CONTAINS:

Preparatory Rhythmic Duos
Vocal and Instrumental Duos
One Choral Cantata excerpt for group singing

Rhythmic Duos

Perform the following preparatory duos intoning the syllable *ta*. Note the various rhythmic levels to be read *before* beginning. Observe the indicated tempi and read at least one measure ahead of the measure being performed. Be aware of the rhythmic content of both parts, your own as well as its counterpart.

---

* Keep in mind that a clef change is usually effected so as to maintain a common tone or small pitch distance (step) at the juncture. Try to anticipate aurally the first note in the new clef.

Minuet

(a)

Andantino

(b)

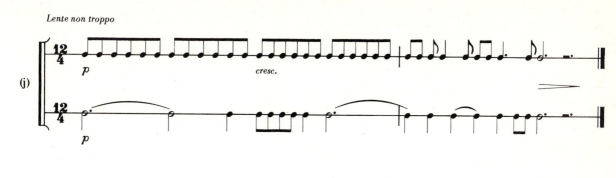

280

Giulio Caccini

281

Heinrich Schütz

282

Luigi Rossi

283

Marin Mersenne

284

Henry Purcell

285

J. K. F. Fischer

286

J. K. F. Fischer

287

Andante

Johann Walther

288

Johann Sebastian Bach

289

Andante lento

Johann Sebastian Bach

290
Minuet

Johann Sebastian Bach

291

Andante

Joseph Haydn

292   Joseph Haydn

Allegro con spirito

293
Allegretto

Wolfgang Amadeus Mozart

Trio*

* Part one only.

294

Ludwig van Beethoven

295

Ludwig van Beethoven

Allegro, ma non troppo

296

Ludwig van Beethoven

297

Slowly

German

Variation I: Minor Mode

Un poco piu mosso

298

Felix Mendelssohn

299

Richard Wagner

Unit Three

Recitatives, Accompanied Songs, and Opera Excerpts from the Seventeenth-, Eighteenth-, and Nineteenth-Century Literature

part F

Recitatives

These recitatives provide material for sightsinging that relates a vocal line to an easily performed, harmonically clear background. The recitatives may·be performed in any of the following ways:

1. Play the accompanying chord progression, noting the relation of the vocal line to the progression and trying to hear it in your mind's ear before singing; then sing the vocal line while playing the supporting chords.
2. Sing the vocal line unaccompanied; then sing the line again adding the accompaniment.
3. Cover the accompanying chords with your hand (or a ruler) and sing the recitative line, being aware of the implied harmonic background as you sing; then compare your interpretation of the implied harmonic background with the actual accompaniment, as you sing the line a second time.
4. Improvise a new vocal line against the given accompaniment.

300
DIDO

Henry Purcell

301

Alessandro Scarlatti

Su le spon-de del Te-bro o-ve le Dee la-ti-ne fe-ce-ro a gl'archi lor cor - - de del cri-ne, co-là, co-la A-min-ta il fi-no da Clo-ri vi-li-pe-so con do-lo-re in-fi-ni-to disse al ciel' disse al mon - do, io, io son tra-di - to!

302

ERMINIO (baritone) / LEONORA (soprano)

(In brac-cio al - la ven-det - ta son tut-ti i sen - si miei.) (Ah, che veg-

ERMINIO / DORALICE (soprano)

g'io Ric - car-do è gui?) (Ma è qui lo scel - le - ra - to.) Ahi

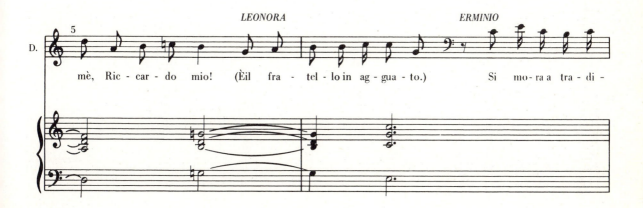

LEONORA / ERMINIO

mè, Ric - car - do mio! (È il fra - tel - lo in ag - gua - to.) Si mo - ra a tra - di -

per l'a-mor, l'af-fet-to che per me a-ve-sti ed hai tem-pra il fu-ror.

ERMINIO

Spie-ta-ta, son for-za-to a ub-bi-dir ti a mio di-spet-to. Ma d'un'

al-ma ir-ri-ta-ta ve-drai, ve-drai l'i-ra che fa. Ca-

RICCARDO

drai, ca-drai pu-ni-to. Non te-me le tue fu-rie un cuo-re ar-di-to.

303

George Frederick Handel

Be-hold! a vir-gin shall con-ceive, and bear a son, and shall call his name Em-man-u-el: God with us.

304

George Frederick Handel

And the an-gel said un-to them, Fear not: for be-

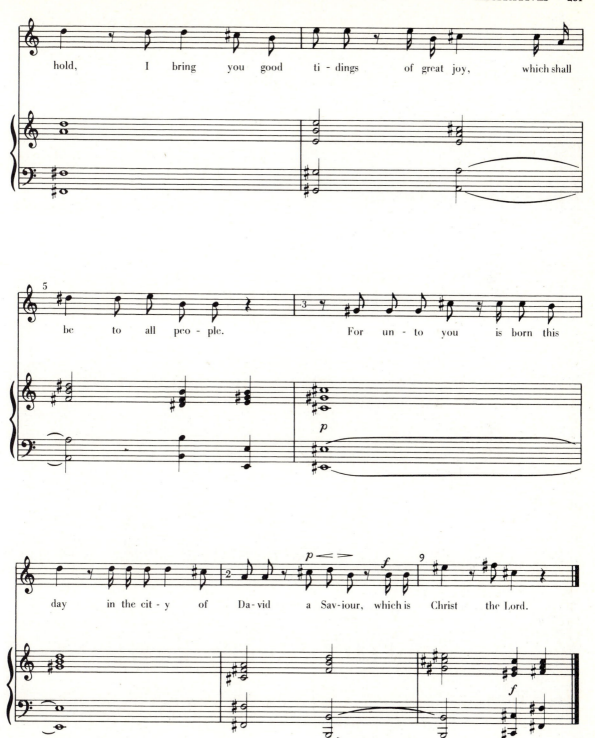

305

George Frederick Handel

Be-hold, I tell you a mys-ter-y; we shall not all sleep, but we shall all be chang'd in a mo-ment, in the twink-ling of an eye, at the last trum-pet.

306

Johann Sebastian Bach

So ste-he denn bei Chri-sti blut-ge färb-ter Fah - ne, o

See - le, —— fest, und glau-be, dass dein Haupt dich nicht ver -

lässt, ja dass sein Sieg auch dir den Weg zu dei-ner Kro - ne

bah - ne. Tritt freu - dig an den

Krieg! Wirst du nur Got-tes Wort so hör-en als be -

307

Johann Sebastian Bach

TENOR

And then did the sol-diers of the gov - ern - or take Je - sus in - to the com-mon

hall, and ga - ther - ed un - to Him the whole band; and strip - ped

Him, and put on Him a scar - let robe; and plait - ed a crown of

thorns, and put it up - on His head, and a reed in his right hand;

308

Tenor

Johann Sebastian Bach

And af-ter they had mock-ed Him, they took off— from— Him the robe, and put His own— gar-ments on Him, and led Him a-way to be— cru - ci-fied. And as they came out, they found a man of Cy-re-ne, whose name was Si-mon; and him com-pel-led they to— bear His Cross.

309

Johann Sebastian Bach

TENOR

He said:

BASS

Go ye in-to the cit-y to such a man, and say to him: The Mas-ter saith to

thee: My time is at hand, I will keep at thy house the Pass-o-ver with my dis-ci-ples.

TENOR

The dis-ci-ples did as Je-sus had ap-point-ed, and made read-y the

310

Joseph Haydn

URIEL.

And God said, Let there be lights in the fir - ma -
ment of heav'n, to di - vide the day from the night, and to give light up - on the
earth; And let them be for signs and for sea - sons, and for days and for
years. He made the stars al - so.

311

Wolfgang Amadeus Mozart

Allegro assai

DONNA ELVIRA

In qua-li ec-ces - si, o

Nu- mi, in qua i mi - sfat-ti or-ri-bi - li, tre-men-di è av - vol-to il scia-gu - ra-to!

Ah no! non

part G

Accompanied Songs

The accompanied songs in this section comprise a sampling of the repertoire from Dowland to Argento. In reading the voice part, the student should attempt first to maintain the pace and rhythm. Either the instructor or another student should read the accompaniment, again aiming to maintain the pace, rhythm and sonority of the piece, even at the expense of details when necessary.

312

John Dowland

313

Larghetto

Carl Maria von Weber

Ein - sam bin ich nicht al - lei - ne, denn__ es schwebt ja süss__ und_ mild_ um mich her__ im Mon - den - schei - ne_ dein ge - lieb - tes, theu - res_ Bild, __ dein__ ge - lieb - tes, __ theu - res_ Bild.

314

Andante

Friedrich Silcher

Franz Schubert

315

Andante

316

Hugo Wolf

In gentle motion

317

Gabriel Pierné

Andante (= 48)

D'un grand mal j'ay l'â-me do-len-te, J'er-re sans con-
Sick my heart and sore-ly in dan-ger, Reft of end or

seil ni des-sein, Brus-lé par u-ne fiè-vre len-te
aim I stray, A fire with a low burn-ing fe-ver

poco rit. *breve* *a tempo*

Qui faist la figue au mé-de-cin. Las! d'a-mour la
That doth the doc-tor e'en dis-may. Ah, by love's un-

Édouard Lalo

318

Andante non troppo

Et par la fe - ne-tre gril - lé - e

Je re - gar - de l'oi - seau joy-eux fen - dant les cieux!

Au - près de lui,

belle es - pé - ran - ce, Por - te - moi sur tes

ai - les d'or, ____ S'il m'aime en - cor, ____

S'il m'aime en - cor!

Et pour en-dor - mir ma souf - fran - ce, Sus - pens mon a - me

sur son coeur ____ Comme u - ne fleur!

319
Moderato

Claude Debussy

L'âme é - va - po - rée   et souf-
fran - te,   L'â - me dou - ce,   l'âme o - do - ran - te Des lis di - vins
que j'ai cueil - lis   Dans   le jar - din   de ta pen - sée,
Où donc les vents l'ont-ils chassée   Cette   âme   a - do - ra - ble des lis?

Dominick Argento

thus sang Gretch-en at her spin - ning wheel.

So might I now sing ev-ery day, for

ev-ery-night I go to bed hop - ing that I shall not wake a-gain, and

each morn-ing on - ly brings back all the sor-rows and grief of the day be - fore.

"Mein - e Ruh' ist

part H

Opera Excerpts

Like the accompanied songs in the preceding section, these opera excerpts pose problems in ensemble coordination that are not encountered in reading single lines. The examples represent a sampling of the opera literature from the seventeenth to the nineteenth centuries. They are appropriate for class performance or for reading with one singer to a part.

321

Claudio Monteverdi

322

Ah   ah, ___   ah,   Be - lin - da,

I   am __   prest __ with __ tor - ment,   Ah,   ah,

ah, _ Be - lin - da, _   I __ am _ prest ____ with tor - ment

would not,   yet would not,   would ____ not have ____ it ____

quess'd. _____

Peace ___ and I   are   stran - gers grown,   Peace ___ and

323

Johann Adam Hiller

Allegretto

DERWIN

Bald _ die Blon - de, bald _ die Brau - ne, bald _ die Mag - re, bald _ die

Di - cke: o _ die wun - der li _ che Lau - ne, o _ der schö - ne Schmet - ter -

Ei - ner einz - gen sanf - ten Bli - cke sich_ mit

p

Seel_ und Leib_ ver - schrei - ben, lass ich gel - ten; doch potz

Vel - ten! Im - mer hin_ und her_ zu trei - ben, im - mer

hin_ und her_ zu trei - ben, ist_ ein gar_ zu-ar - ges Ding, ist_ ein

gar - zu ar - ges Ding; im - mer hin — und her — zu trei - ben, im - mer

hin — und her — zu trei - ben, ist — ein gar — zu ar - ges

Ding, ist — ein gar — zu ar - ges Ding.

324

Ludwig van Beethoven

ROCCO (baritone)

325

Giacomo Puccini

Un poco piu mosso ♩ = 126

Materials from the Twentieth-Century Repertoire

These materials present problems representative of contemporary music in the most general sense. Many of the examples by more traditional twentieth-century composers such as Bartók, Hindemith, and Stravinsky reveal characteristics of style easily associated with music of the previous (common practice) era. On the other hand, some of the examples by Schoenberg, Webern, Messiaen, and others reveal few real semblances of tonality or unambiguously metrical rhythm. In approaching this music, the reader will find it more fruitful, as a rule, to strive for *intervallic* accuracy rather than seeking pitch relations within a key. Moreover, attention to details of articulation, phrasing and dynamics can add a dimension to sightsinging that is not achieved in terms of pitch and rhythm alone.

part I

Melodies and Duos from the
Concert Literature

Rhythmic Drill

The rhythmic exercises that follow present a sampling of procedures that have become part and parcel of the music of the current century. These include mixed (or changing) meter (example 1), non-accentual or ametric rhythms (exercise 9), irregular beat divisions (exercise 13), and a variety of rhythmic groupings into patterns that involve displaced accents (exercises 1, 3, 4 and 7), or combinations thereof (exercise 6).

In most cases mastery of these rhythms will involve considerable practice, so that students are urged to follow the routine mapped below:

1. Scan each example for tempo, meter, and meter changes.
2. Tap or conduct the meter(s) of the example.
3. Scan each example for the kinds of note durations used, their grouping into patterns (especially where accents are concerned), the use of dynamics, fermata and other interpretive signs.
4. Intone the rhythm while tapping or conducting the meter; break the example into segments, then connect the segments and perform the entire example.

Aaron Copeland

Igor Stravinsky

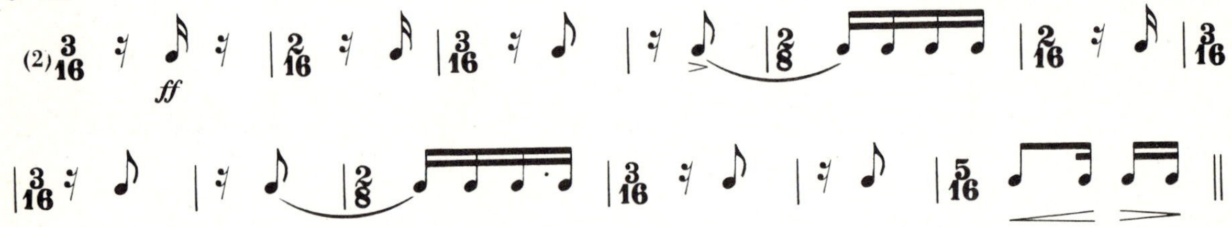

Aaron Copeland

Igor Stravinsky

Elliott Carter

Igor Stravinsky

Olivier Messiaen

Arnold Schoenberg

György Ligeti

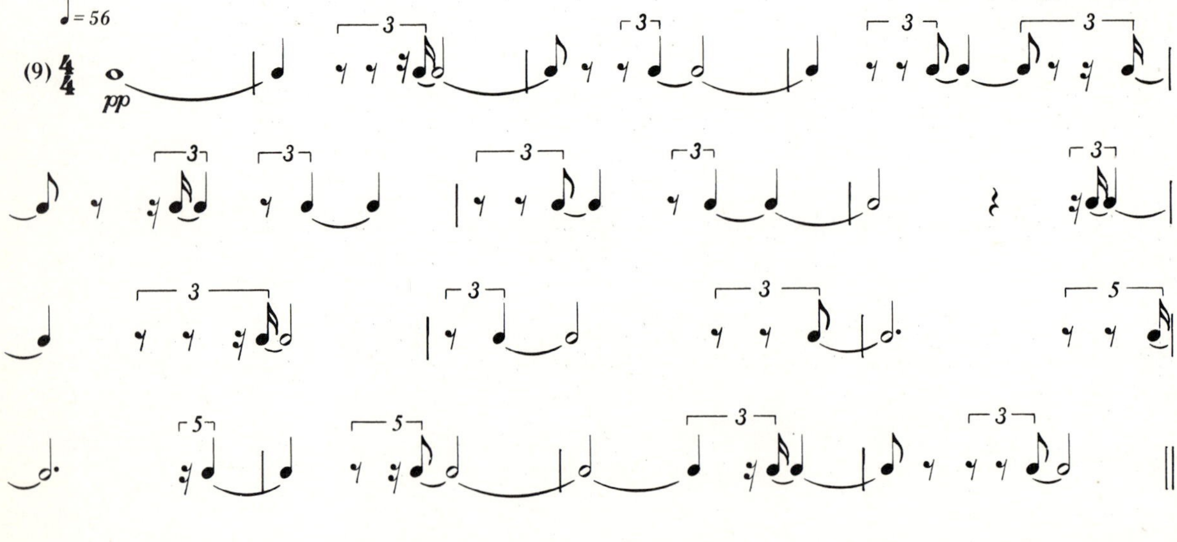

Béla Bartók

Anton Webern

Elliott Carter

Bruno Maderna

327

Claude Debussy

328

Largo

Charles Ives

329

Evenly and mechanically

Charles Ives

330

Arnold Schoenberg

Alegro molto, energico

* All notes not marked with sharp or flat are natural.

The duet that follows is based on an octatonic scale. Sing the scale preparatory to reading the duet.

Octatonic Scale

334

Béla Bartók

338

Béla Bartók

Lento, ♩ = 72

339

Igor Stravinsky

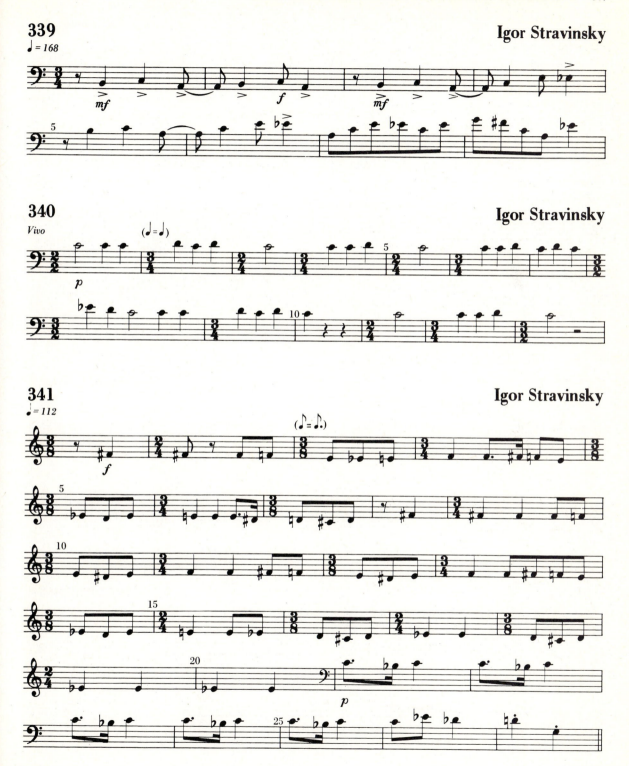

340

Igor Stravinsky

341

Igor Stravinsky

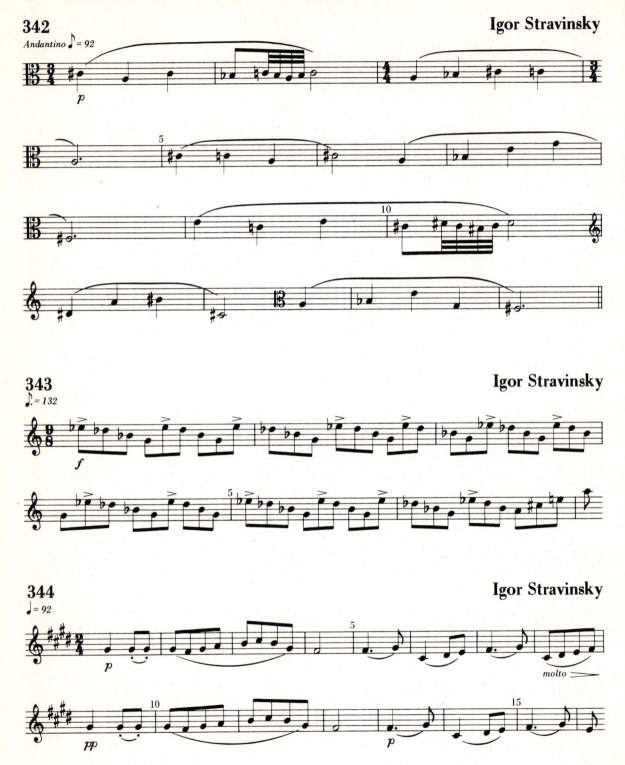

345

Anton Webern

Sehr lebhaft

346

Anton Webern

Sehr lebhaft

347

Alban Berg

348

Paul Hindemith

349

Paul Hindemith

350

Paul Hindemith

Flowing

351   **Luigi Dallapiccola**

352   **Elliott Carter**

Misterioso (Tempo rubato)

353   **Dmitri Shostakovich**

Largo

354

♩ = 160

Dmitri Shostakovich

355

Lukas Foss

356

Olivier Messiaen

Au mouvement

simile

* Retain a common rhythmic unit, here the shortest recurring duration (♪), as a basis for accurately relating the various note durations. Intone the rhythm alone before singing the melody.

part J

Melodies, Duos, and Adaptations for Improvisation from Jazz and Popular Music

The materials that follow pose a variety of sightreading problems. The main function of these examples is to challenge students who have not previously dealt with the jazz or popular idioms, and who need to broaden their reading capabilities through exposure to problems that are idiosyncratic to jazz. There is sufficient material here as well to challenge the student who has had prior exposure to the pop and jazz idioms.

PART J CONTAINS:

1. Unaccompanied popular melodies (*The Sound of Silence*).
2. Jazz duo arrangements based on well-known popular tunes (*Blue Moon* or *'S Wonderful*).
3. Blues, with cued-in chord changes for a pianist or guitarist, suitable for improvised choruses.
4. Improvisations on standard jazz tunes, with accompanying chord symbols for improvised choruses.

The Sound of Silence

Paul Simon

I'll Never Fall in Love Again

Burt Bacharach

Blue Moon

359

Swinging

Promises, Promises

360

Burt Bacharach

In the Mode

361

Big Red Blues

362

Blue Riffin

363

Variation on Body and Soul

364

Moderately slow

Blues in Gee . . .

Scotch Nap

Up, Up and Away

367

Jimmy Webb

Moderately

Would you like to ride in my beau-ti-ful bal-loon?
world's a nic-er place in my beau-ti-ful bal-loon. It
Love is wait-ing there in my beau-ti-ful bal-loon.

Would you like to glide in my beau-ti-ful bal-loon? We could float
wears a nic-er face in my beau-ti-ful bal-loon. We can sing
Way up in the air in my beau-ti-ful bal-loon. If you'll hold

a-mong the stars to-geth-er you and I,
a song and sail a-long the sil-ver sky, For we can fly!
my hand we'll chase your dream a-cross the sky,

We can fly!

Up, up and a-way, my beau-ti-ful my beau-ti-ful bal-loon!

To next strain — *Fine* — *Repeat and fade*

The

Sus-pend-ed un-der a twi-light can-o-py

We'll search the clouds for a star to guide us.

If by some chance you find your-self lov-ing me, We'll

find a cloud to hide us, Keep the moon be-side us.

D.C. al Fine

Blues Improvisation

368

Charlie Parker

Improvisation based on: *All the Things You Are*

Jerome Kern

Jazz Duo and Improvisation on Gershwin's:
'S Wonderful

George Gershwin

370
Moderately fast

Bacharach Variations

371

Swinging

Burt Bacharach

Sing the following improvised solo as played by Miles Davis on Capitol record
DT-1974: *Venus De Milo* (Gerry Mulligan).

372

Gerry Mulligan

With a lift

Appendix
Supplementary Exercises

The exercises in this appendix may be used:

1. As preparation for music literature presenting related problems.
2. Where a lack of success in reading the examples from literature suggests a need for additional preparation.
3. As a separate, relatively complete unit of exercises to be mastered before beginning the examples in a particular unit of the text. Instructors and students are encouraged to devise similar additional exercises as needed.

Exercise 1

Interpreting Scale Degrees

Sing the following series of numbers by equating each number to the scale degree that it represents in the given key. Note that 8 designates the upper tonic while 1 denotes a lower tonic. The succession 7–8 denotes leading tone to tonic in the upper octave while 7–1 signifies the lower leading tone to tonic.

SAMPLE: SING (ON NUMBER) THE FOLLOWING PATTERN IN D MAJOR; SOUND THE TONIC BEFORE BEGINNING.

1 2 3 5 4 5 6 7 5 7 8 6 5 2 4 3 2 1

SING EACH OF THE FOLLOWING SERIES FORWARDS AND/OR BACKWARDS.

(a) F major: 1 3 2 4 3 5 6 7 8 5 3 6 5 7 1 3 5 1.
(b) E minor:* 1 2 3 1 5 6 5 8 7 6 5 1 4 3 2 7♯ 1 3 5 6 5 3 1.
(c) Eb major: 5 6 7 8 4 8 3 8 2 8 1 2 4 3 6 5 7 8 1.
(d) D major: 1 2 3 1 4 5 3 1 5 6 7 5 8 6 5 1 4 3 1 3 1.
(e) C minor: 1 3 5 6 5 3 4 2 1 3 6 7 6 5 8 7♮ 8 7♮ 6♮ 5 7♮ 8 1.
(f) Db major: 5 3 6 4 3 2 5 1 8 4 7 3 6 5 4 2 7 8 1 7 8 2 1.
(g) A minor: 8 7 6 5 8 4 5 6 5 7♯ 5 7♮ 6 5 3 4 2♭ 1 7 1.
(h) C major: 1 3 5 7 8 6 3 4 5 3 5 7 2 7 8 3 7 2 6 1 7 1.
(i) C-sharp major: 1 2 4 3 5 4 7 8 6 8 5 4 8 3 2 7 1 8 7 8.
(j) G major: 5 3 1 8 7 8 6 8 5 4 8 3 2 7 8 1 7 5 4 7 1.

* Denotes natural minor.

Exercise 2

Relative Scale Patterns for Major and Minor Keys

Sound the tonic and relate the beginning and ending degrees to the tonic before singing. Intone on fixed *do* or *la*.

Exercise 3

Practice Melodies Containing Steps and Thirds:
Major and Minor Modes

Exercise 4

Step Progression

Step connections in the form of structurally important major or minor seconds, form the basis for most melodies and voice leading in tonal music. In example 1, successive on-the-beat steps provide a simple, scalar framework for melodic detail: the accompanying leaps can be heard as embellishments of a skeletal series of step progressions. Awareness of underlying step progressions, as graphed below, can provide a basis for reading ahead and for organizing a melodic line in a patterned series of goals.

Sing the step progressions graphed for each of the melodies in exercise 4, then sing the melodies using the notes of the step progressions as points of reference.

(a)

(b)

(c)

Johann Sebastian Bach

(d)

Giovanni da Palestrina

(e)

Josquin des Prez

(f)

Exercise 5

Interval Practice for Fourths and Fifths

Step motion is the core of most melodic activity. However, step motion can be balanced and linear variety added by disjunct motion or leaps. For example, performing the ascending fourth, G to C, is facilitated by singing the intervening steps to A and B as a means of connecting G to C. Next think, but do not sing the intervening steps so that you connect the tones forming the leap with your mind's hear.

o ca. 60

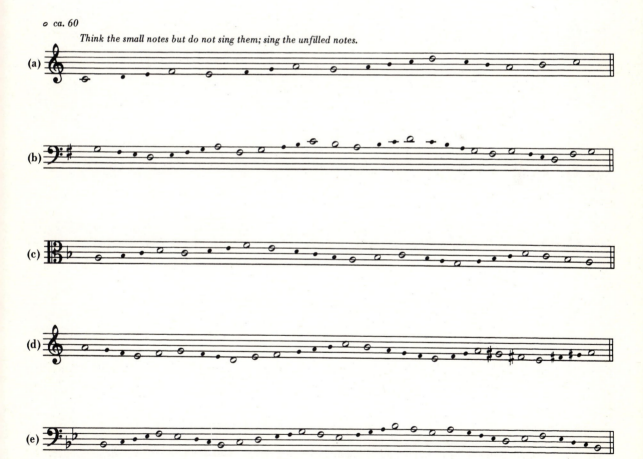

Exercise 6

Relating Leaps to Patterns

Leaps are often heard in patterns involving three notes: a leap followed by a rising or falling step. For this reason leaps can frequently be given clearer tonal definition if the note following the leap is heard as a goal, or note of resolution of the leap itself.

In the following exercises, try to hear each leap in relation to or as a kind of appoggiatura to the note of resolution. Perform each pattern as follows:

1. Sing (on note names) the pitches that precede and follow the leap.
2. Sing the complete pattern, directing the leap in your mind's ear toward the note of resolution.

Exercise 7

Melodic Interval Drills

THIRDS

FOURTHS

FIFTHS AND SIXTHS

SIXTHS AND SEVENTHS

Exercise 8

Chord Outlines: Intervals

In music in which melody and harmony are interdependent, melodic leaps frequently reflect chord outlining or arpeggiation. The leap can be heard as part of a chord which is in turn the basis for an accompanying chord:

Play the chord and sing the melodic interval, noting the relation between the chord and the melodic pitches. Sing in your own voice range regardless of the clef used.

(a)

(b)

(c)

Exercise 9

Chord Outlines: Triads

Read in both major and parallel minor forms.

Intone *   C   E   G   E   C

* Intone on *note-names*.

Exercise 10

Chord Progressions for Vocalization

Sing the upper line in your voice register while playing the bass on the piano (or any appropriate bass instrument). Be aware of chord functions as you read.

Exercise 11

Chord Singing on Major-Minor Seventh Chords

The four chords outlined melodically on each stave form a series of root position or inverted major-minor seventh chords. The chords are linked by a common tone, marked with a circle. Using the common tones as reference pitches, sing through each stave without pause. Sing on note names or chord members, for example, NNN.

o = ca. 80

Exercise 12

Melodic Patterns Based on the Dominant Seventh

Sing on la

Exercise 13

Aural Completion of Chord Tones

Play the unfilled notes and *sing* the filled (blackened) note.

(a)

(b)

(c)

(d)

Exercise 14

Play and Sing

Patterns based on the chromatic scale to be sung against one sustained note.

♩ = *ca. 120*

Exercise 15

Compound Intervals

Compound intervals represent octave extensions of simple intervals. A major ninth (M9) amounts to a M2 plus an octave, a major tenth is formed by a M3 plus an octave and a perfect eleventh (p. 11) consists of a perfect fourth plus an octave. Although there are no *theoretical* limits to the nomenclature of compound intervals, practical considerations, particularly vocal limitations, are such that intervals larger than the P 15 (two octaves) are not given precise description in common practice, nor, as a rule, are they observed in vocal sightreading. The generally observed compound intervals are as follows:

The smaller compound intervals, ninths and tenths, are by far the most common, and the exercises that follow reflect this practice.

Preparatory Exercise in Singing Compound Intervals

1. Play the first note of each pair or group and then sing the pattern (in a comfortable register).

2. Sing each interval or pattern, maintaining a steady pace (ca. o= MM 80).

Exercise 16

Pitch Exercise in Modular 12

In Mod. 12 (Modular Twelve), all twelve notes of a chromatic scale are related to a starting or *reference* pitch in terms of the number of semitones that constitute their distance from the reference note. The reference note is designated 0, and the remaining eleven notes of the chromatic scale are named (0) 1 2 3 4 5 6 7 8 9 10 11, accounting for all of the available pitches (pitch classes or p.c.'s) within an octave:

Each note's digit defines the number of *semitones* separating it from (0 C**) In practice, any note may serve as the reference pitch or starting note, but in the drills presented here only the pitch class C is used as the reference pitch.

Mod. 12 is particularly useful as a tool for naming or intoning pitch where tonality or key feeling is not operative, and where diatonic key organization is replaced by a twelve note complement of pitches. This is the case in a great deal of the music of this century.

Practice applying Mod. 12 nomenclature to a chromatic scale on C and to pitch patterns derived from it; then proceed to the sample drills that follow.

* Note that enharmonic equivalents are *not* differentiated in Mod. 12.

** The semitones are counted *above* O only.

Sing this scale using Mod. 12 as shown.

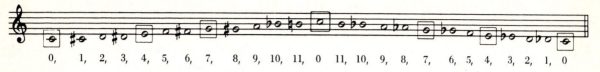

0, 1, 2, 3, 4, 5, 6, 7, 8, 9, 10, 11, 0 11, 10, 9, 8, 7, 6, 5, 4, 3, 2, 1, 0

Sing these pitch patterns using Mod. 12 as shown.

(a)

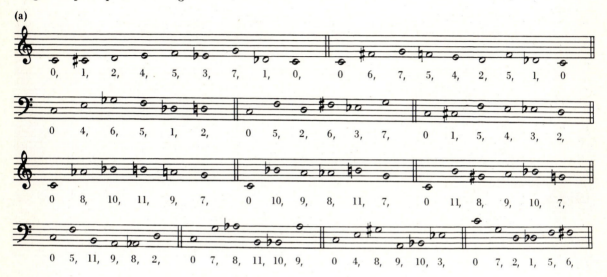

0, 1, 2, 4, 5, 3, 7, 1, 0,   0 6, 7, 5, 4, 2, 5, 1, 0

0 4, 6, 5, 1, 2,   0 5, 2, 6, 3, 7,   0 1, 5, 4, 3, 2,

0 8, 10, 11, 9, 7,   0 10, 9, 8, 11, 7,   0 11, 8, 9, 10, 7,

0 5, 11, 9, 8, 2,   0 7, 8, 11, 10, 9,   0 4, 8, 9, 10, 3,   0 7, 2, 1, 5, 6,

Sing these intervals using Mod. 12 based on C.

(b)

Sing 0, 4

Sing these 3-note patterns in Mod. 12 based on C.

(c)

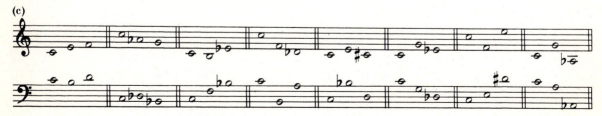

Sing the following pitch groups in Mod. 12.

(d)

Play one line and sing the other in Mod. 12; reverse the procedure.

(e)

Sing the following pitch sets using Mod. 12 based on *C.*...

(f)

Arnold Schoenberg

Arnold Schoenberg

Anton Webern

Igor Stravinsky

Arnold Schoenberg

Hans Werner

Igor Stravinsky

Arnold Schoenberg

TEMPO AND EXPRESSION TERMS

Abbandono, with abandon
Adagietto, somewhat slow
Adagio, very slow
Affettuoso, with feeling
Agitato, agitated
Aimable, good-naturedly
Alla, in the style of
Allegretto, moderately fast
Allegro, fast
Amoroso, lovingly
Andante, moderately slow
Andantino, somewhat faster than *andante*
Animato, spirited
Anmut, with grace
A piacere, freely
Appassionata, impassioned
A tempo, in original tempo
Ausdruckvoll, expressive
Ben, well, very
Bewegt, agitated
Breit, broadly
Brio, brilliance
Calore, warmth
Cantabile, in a singing style
Caressant, caressingly
Cedez, yielding
Chaleur, warmth
Commodo, easy-going tempo
Con, with (used with other terms)
Deciso, decidedly
Dolce, soft, sweet
Dolente, sad
Einfach, simply
Energico, energetically
Espressivo, expressive
Etwas, somewhat (used with other terms)
Feierlich, solemn
Fervore, fervor

Frei, free
Fröhlich, happy
Gai, gay
Gefühl, feeling
Gemächlich, leisurely
Gesangvoll, in a singing style
Geschwind, quick
Giocoso, humorously
Giusto, strict
Grandioso, with pomp
Grave, solemn, slow
Grazioso, gracefully
Innig, fervent, heartfelt
Klagend, mournfully
Kraftig, strong
Langoureux, languishing
Langsam, slow
Largamente, in a broad style
Larghetto, slower than *andante*
Largo, very slow and broad
Lebendig, vivacious
Leggiero, light, airy
Leise, soft, gentle
Lento, slow
Lieblich, in a loving manner
Lusingando, soft, coaxing
Lustig, cheerful
Mächtig, powerful
Maestoso, majestic
Marcato, decisively
Marziale, in march style
Mässig, moderate
Mazurka, mazurka
Meno, less (used with other terms)
Minuetto, minuet tempo
Molto, much, very
Mosso, motion
Nicht, not (used with other terms)

Pesante, loud and heavy
Piacere, freely in tempo
Più, more (used with other terms)
Poco, a little (used with other terms)
Pomposo, pompously
Presto, fast
Primo, first
Quasi, in the manner of, about
Rallentando, slowing down
Rasch, fast
Religioso, in a religious style
Risoluto, firm, resolute
Scherzando, scherzoso, playfully
Schnell, fast, rapidly
Sehnsuchtvoll, full of longing
Semplice, simply
Sempre, always (used with other terms)
Singend, lyrically
Smorzando, dying away
Sospirando, sighing
Sostenuto, sustained
Spiritoso, spirited
Stark, strong
Suave, agreeable, sweet
Subito, suddenly
Tanto, much
Teneramente, tenderly
Tenuto, hold (a single note)
Tranquillo, quietly, peacefully
Träumerisch, dreamy
Triste, sadly
Troppo, too much
Vif, Vivace, Vivo,
Vite, quick, lively
Vigoroso, vigorous
Zart, gently, tenderly
Ziemlich, somewhat

Acknowledgments
(continued from copyright page)

Index of Musical Examples

*Author's.

*Author's .